"After utilizing toolkits from The Art of S
threats within my organization to which I w
my team's knowledge as a competitive advantage, we now have superior
systems that save time and energy."

"As a new Chief Technology Officer, I was feeling unprepared and inadequate to be successful in my role. I ordered an IT toolkit Sunday night and was prepared Monday morning to shed light on areas of improvement within my organization. I no longer felt overwhelmed and intimidated, I was excited to share what I had learned."

"I used the questionnaires to interview members of my team. I never knew how many insights we could produce collectively with our internal knowledge."

"I usually work until at least 8pm on weeknights. The Art of Service questionnaire saved me so much time and worry that Thursday night I attended my son's soccer game without sacrificing my professional obligations."

"After purchasing The Art of Service toolkit, I was able to identify areas where my company was not in compliance that could have put my job at risk. I looked like a hero when I proactively educated my team on the risks and presented a solid solution."

"I spent months shopping for an external consultant before realizing that The Art of Service would allow my team to consult themselves! Not only did we save time not catching a consultant up to speed, we were able to keep our company information and industry secrets confidential."

"Everyday there are new regulations and processes in my industry. The Art of Service toolkit has kept me ahead by using AI technology to constantly update the toolkits and address emerging needs."

"I customized The Art of Service toolkit to focus specifically on the concerns of my role and industry. I didn't have to waste time with a generic self-help book that wasn't tailored to my exact situation."

"Many of our competitors have asked us about our secret sauce. When I tell them it's the knowledge we have in-house, they never believe me. Little do they know The Art of Service toolkits are working behind the scenes."

"One of my friends hired a consultant who used the knowledge gained working with his company to advise their competitor. Talk about a competitive disadvantage! The Art of Service allowed us to keep our knowledge from walking out the door along with a huge portion of our budget in consulting fees."

"Honestly, I didn't know what I didn't know. Before purchasing The Art of Service, I didn't realize how many areas of my business needed to be refreshed and improved. I am so relieved The Art of Service was there to highlight our blind spots."

"Before The Art of Service, I waited eagerly for consulting company reports to come out each month. These reports kept us up to speed but provided little value because they put our competitors on the same playing field. With The Art of Service, we have uncovered unique insights to drive our business forward."

"Instead of investing extensive resources into an external consultant, we can spend more of our budget towards pursuing our company goals and objectives...while also spending a little more on corporate holiday parties."

"The risk of our competitors getting ahead has been mitigated because The Art of Service has provided us with a 360-degree view of threats within our organization before they even arise."

ISO 20000
Complete Self-Assessment Guide

https://theartofservice.com
support@theartofservice.com

Table of Contents

About The Art of Service

The Art of Service, Business Process Architects since 2000, is dedicated to helping stakeholders achieve excellence.

Defining, designing, creating, and implementing a process to solve a stakeholders challenge or meet an objective is the most valuable role… In EVERY group, company, organization and department.

Unless you're talking a one-time, single-use project, there should be a process. Whether that process is managed and implemented by humans, AI, or a combination of the two, it needs to be designed by someone with a complex enough perspective to ask the right questions.

Someone capable of asking the right questions and step back and say, 'What are we really trying to accomplish here? And is there a different way to look at it?'

With The Art of Service's Self-Assessments, we empower people who can do just that — whether their title is marketer, entrepreneur, manager, salesperson, consultant, Business Process Manager, executive assistant, IT Manager, CIO etc... —they are the people who rule the future. They are people who watch the process as it happens, and ask the right questions to make the process work better.

Contact us when you need any support with this Self-Assessment and any help with templates, blue-prints and examples of standard documents you might need:

https://theartofservice.com
support@theartofservice.com

Included Resources - how to access

Included with your purchase of the book is the ISO 20000

Self-Assessment Spreadsheet Dashboard which contains all questions and Self-Assessment areas and auto-generates insights, graphs, and project RACI planning - all with examples to get you started right away.

How? Simply send an email to
access@theartofservice.com
with this books' title in the subject to get the ISO 20000 Self Assessment Tool right away.

The auto reply will guide you further, you will then receive the following contents with New and Updated specific criteria:

- The latest quick edition of the book in PDF
- The latest complete edition of the book in PDF, which criteria correspond to the criteria in...
- The Self-Assessment Excel Dashboard, and...
- Example pre-filled Self-Assessment Excel Dashboard to get familiar with results generation
- In-depth specific Checklists covering the topic
- Project management checklists and templates to assist with implementation

INCLUDES LIFETIME SELF ASSESSMENT UPDATES

Every self assessment comes with Lifetime Updates and Lifetime Free Updated Books. Lifetime Updates is an industry-first feature which allows you to receive verified self assessment updates, ensuring you always have the most accurate information at your fingertips.

Get it now- you will be glad you did - do it now, before you forget.

Send an email to **access@theartofservice.com** with this books' title in the subject to get the ISO 20000 Self Assessment Tool right away.

Purpose of this Self-Assessment

This Self-Assessment has been developed to improve understanding of the requirements and elements of ISO 20000, based on best practices and standards in business process architecture, design and quality management.

It is designed to allow for a rapid Self-Assessment to determine how closely existing management practices and procedures correspond to the elements of the Self-Assessment.

The criteria of requirements and elements of ISO 20000 have been rephrased in the format of a Self-Assessment questionnaire, with a seven-criterion scoring system, as explained in this document.

In this format, even with limited background knowledge of ISO 20000, a manager can quickly review existing operations to determine how they measure up to the standards. This in turn can serve as the starting point of a 'gap analysis' to identify management tools or system elements that might usefully be implemented in the organization to help improve overall performance.

How to use the Self-Assessment

On the following pages are a series of questions to identify to what extent your ISO 20000 initiative is complete in comparison to the requirements set in standards.

To facilitate answering the questions, there is a space in front of each question to enter a score on a scale of '1' to '5'.

1 Strongly Disagree

2 Disagree

3 Neutral

4 Agree

5 Strongly Agree

Read the question and rate it with the following in front of mind:

**'In my belief,
the answer to this question is clearly defined'.**

There are two ways in which you can choose to interpret this statement;

1. how aware are you that the answer to the question is clearly defined
2. for more in-depth analysis you can choose to gather evidence and confirm the answer to the question. This obviously will take more time, most Self-Assessment users opt for the first way to interpret the question and dig deeper later on based on the outcome of the overall Self-Assessment.

A score of '1' would mean that the answer is not clear at all, where a '5' would mean the answer is crystal clear and defined. Leave emtpy when the question is not applicable or you don't want to answer it, you can skip it without affecting your score. Write your score in the space provided.

After you have responded to all the appropriate statements in each section, compute your average score for that section, using the formula provided, and round to the nearest tenth. Then transfer to the corresponding spoke in the ISO 20000 Scorecard on the second next page of the Self-Assessment.

Your completed ISO 20000 Scorecard will give you a clear presentation of which ISO 20000 areas need attention.

ISO 20000 Scorecard Example

Example of how the finalized Scorecard can look like:

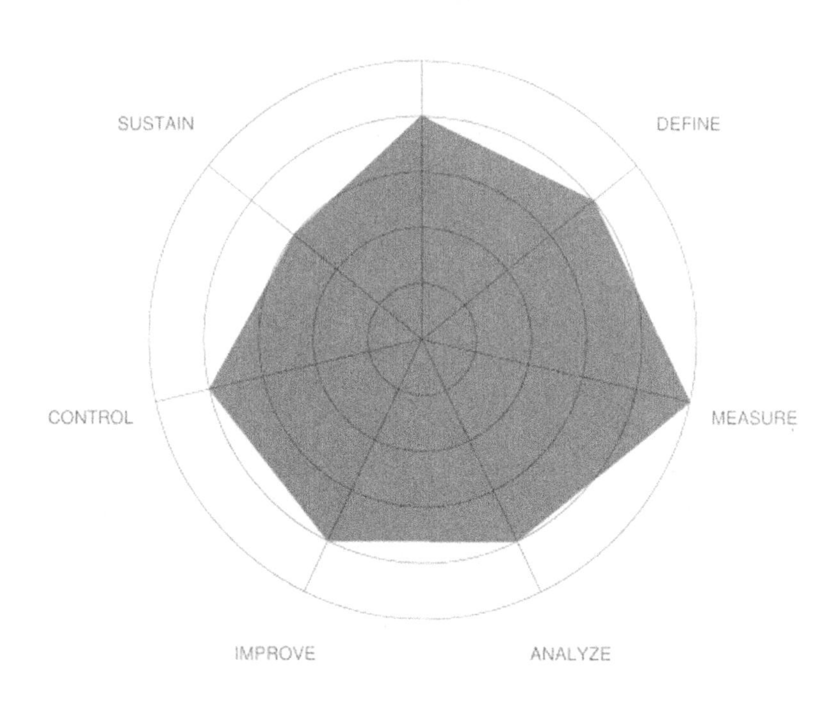

ISO 20000 Scorecard

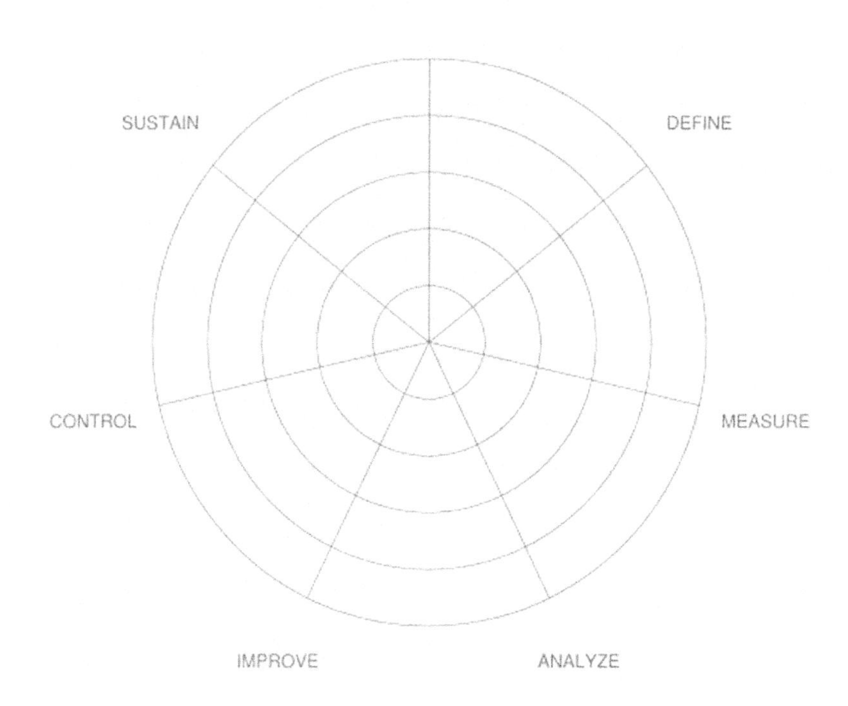

BEGINNING OF THE SELF-ASSESSMENT:

CRITERION #1: RECOGNIZE

INTENT: Be aware of the need for change. Recognize that there is an unfavorable variation, problem or symptom.

In my belief, the answer to this question is clearly defined:

5 Strongly Agree

4 Agree

3 Neutral

2 Disagree

1 Strongly Disagree

1. What training and capacity building actions are needed to implement proposed reforms?
<--- Score

2. Who is responsible for Problem Management?
<--- Score

3. What needs to change in your organization?
<--- Score

4. Think about the people you identified for your ISO 20000 project and the project responsibilities you would assign to them, what kind of training do you think they would need to perform these responsibilities effectively?
<--- Score

5. Consider your own ISO 20000 project, what types of organizational problems do you think might be causing or affecting your problem, based on the work done so far?
<--- Score

6. What are the main issues leading to customer dissatisfaction?
<--- Score

7. What extra resources will you need?
<--- Score

8. What other things are needed products and services?
<--- Score

9. How is everyone going to work together to do what is needed?
<--- Score

10. Do you need all the bells and whistles all the time?
<--- Score

11. Do you have an employee association that is recognized by management?
<--- Score

12. Are controls defined to recognize and contain problems?
<--- Score

13. What problems are you facing and how do you consider ISO 20000 will circumvent those obstacles?
<--- Score

14. Are all employees involved in incident and service request management able to access and use relevant information to help resolve issues or successfully respond to the request?
<--- Score

15. What would happen if ISO 20000 weren't done?
<--- Score

16. To what extent does each concerned units management team recognize ISO 20000 as an effective investment?
<--- Score

17. How many of the users will need access from remote?
<--- Score

18. Do you know what you need to know about ISO 20000?
<--- Score

19. Are you dealing with any of the same issues today as yesterday? What can you do about this?
<--- Score

20. Do you identify new and changing service

requirements?
<--- Score

21. What is needed to promote biogas digester?
<--- Score

22. What situation(s) led to this ISO 20000 Self Assessment?
<--- Score

23. Did you feel the need for a specialized software tool?
<--- Score

24. Can demand management be used to avoid the need to carry out any tuning?
<--- Score

25. What is change management and why is it needed?
<--- Score

26. What does ISO 20000 success mean to the stakeholders?
<--- Score

27. What are the expected benefits of ISO 20000 to the stakeholder?
<--- Score

28. How much are sponsors, customers, partners, stakeholders involved in ISO 20000? In other words, what are the risks, if ISO 20000 does not deliver successfully?
<--- Score

29. How are the ISO 20000's objectives aligned to the group's overall stakeholder strategy?
<--- Score

30. What are the statutory and legal requirements the service provider needs to take into account?
<--- Score

31. What ISO 20000 problem should be solved?
<--- Score

32. What prevents you from making the changes you know will make you a more effective ISO 20000 leader?
<--- Score

33. What are the stakeholder objectives to be achieved with ISO 20000?
<--- Score

34. How are you going to measure success?
<--- Score

35. Where do you need to exercise leadership?
<--- Score

36. Have you identified your ISO 20000 key performance indicators?
<--- Score

37. What ISO 20000 coordination do you need?
<--- Score

38. Is your it department getting enough information in order to support strategic business needs?

<--- Score

39. Why is relationship management needed?
<--- Score

40. How does the project fulfil the urgent target group needs?
<--- Score

41. Who needs what information?
<--- Score

42. What are the issues for an internal user of a purchasing department that are indicative of high levels of service quality?
<--- Score

43. Which information does the ISO 20000 business case need to include?
<--- Score

44. Who else hopes to benefit from it?
<--- Score

45. What difference does your organization make, the argument went, around a problem so vast as climate change?
<--- Score

46. Who defines the rules in relation to any given issue?
<--- Score

47. What are the basic steps in your organization special needs adoption?
<--- Score

48. What is the portfolio of services that is needed to meet service requirements?
<--- Score

49. Do you recognize ISO 20000 achievements?
<--- Score

50. Are there any revenue recognition issues?
<--- Score

51. Have you ever thought about being prevented from accessing and using your own information?
<--- Score

52. Are employees recognized or rewarded for performance that demonstrates the highest levels of integrity?
<--- Score

53. What benefits and outcomes do you need?
<--- Score

54. Are there any specific expectations or concerns about the ISO 20000 team, ISO 20000 itself?
<--- Score

55. Who needs to know?
<--- Score

56. What should be considered when identifying available resources, constraints, and deadlines?
<--- Score

57. Do you find that ITIL / ISO 20000 have fulfilled your needs?

<--- Score

58. What are the ISO 20000 resources needed?
<--- Score

59. What information do users need?
<--- Score

60. Has the immediate need been resolved through Change or Incident Management?
<--- Score

61. Have patch management requirements been identified and responsible support groups notified?
<--- Score

62. What problems typically occur in an ISO 20000 project?
<--- Score

63. What are the customer and business requirements, needs and expectations?
<--- Score

64. What are your needs in relation to ISO 20000 skills, labor, equipment, and markets?
<--- Score

65. Do you use your mechanism to identify service requirements?
<--- Score

66. How do you demonstrate your it services are managed to meet your business needs?
<--- Score

67. As a sponsor, customer or management, how important is it to meet goals, objectives?
<--- Score

68. What do employees need in the short term?
<--- Score

69. Which factors trigger the release management?
<--- Score

Add up total points for this section:
_____ = Total points for this section

Divided by: ______ (number of statements answered) = ______ Average score for this section

Transfer your score to the ISO 20000 Index at the beginning of the Self-Assessment.

CRITERION #2: DEFINE:

INTENT: Formulate the stakeholder problem. Define the problem, needs and objectives.

In my belief, the answer to this question is clearly defined:

5 Strongly Agree

4 Agree

3 Neutral

2 Disagree

1 Strongly Disagree

1. Have the customer needs been translated into specific, measurable requirements? How?
<--- Score

2. What would be the goal or target for a ISO 20000's improvement team?
<--- Score

3. Is there a definition of a service complaint and a

procedure to manage and escalate any that arise?
<--- Score

4. What are the contractual requirements?
<--- Score

5. What are the dynamics of the communication plan?
<--- Score

6. Do the problem and goal statements meet the SMART criteria (specific, measurable, attainable, relevant, and time-bound)?
<--- Score

7. Does the program define specific measurement and success criteria?
<--- Score

8. What knowledge or experience is required?
<--- Score

9. What sources do you use to gather information for a ISO 20000 study?
<--- Score

10. Has the ISO 20000 work been fairly and/or equitably divided and delegated among team members who are qualified and capable to perform the work? Has everyone contributed?
<--- Score

11. Does a release cover installations required by a service request handling?
<--- Score

12. Have specific policy objectives been defined?

<--- Score

13. What are the requirements of the legislation?
<--- Score

14. What specifically is the problem? Where does it occur? When does it occur? What is its extent?
<--- Score

15. Has the direction changed at all during the course of ISO 20000? If so, when did it change and why?
<--- Score

16. Has/have the customer(s) been identified?
<--- Score

17. Do you clarify how the term service complaint is defined?
<--- Score

18. When is the estimated completion date?
<--- Score

19. How many applications are critical and require security assessment?
<--- Score

20. Did the project require purchase or lease of equipment or commodities?
<--- Score

21. Are the ISO 20000 requirements testable?
<--- Score

22. Do you respond to new and changing service requirements?

<--- Score

23. What happens if ISO 20000's scope changes?
<--- Score

24. Are team charters developed?
<--- Score

25. Do you include or refer to the scope of service delivery activities?
<--- Score

26. Are there any constraints known that bear on the ability to perform ISO 20000 work? How is the team addressing them?
<--- Score

27. Are roles and responsibilities formally defined?
<--- Score

28. Has everyone on the team, including the team leaders, been properly trained?
<--- Score

29. Are improvement team members fully trained on ISO 20000?
<--- Score

30. Are customers identified and high impact areas defined?
<--- Score

31. How was the 'as is' process map developed, reviewed, verified and validated?
<--- Score

32. What are the continuous compliance requirements?
<--- Score

33. Have all basic functions of ISO 20000 been defined?
<--- Score

34. What characteristics are required for load to provide reliability services?
<--- Score

35. How release management activities are performed in the case organization?
<--- Score

36. Should an sla define what the customer wants or what you can measure?
<--- Score

37. Why are some loads a particularly good match for power system reliability requirements?
<--- Score

38. If substitutes have been appointed, have they been briefed on the ISO 20000 goals and received regular communications as to the progress to date?
<--- Score

39. What is a worst-case scenario for losses?
<--- Score

40. Will team members perform ISO 20000 work when assigned and in a timely fashion?
<--- Score

41. Are the adoption requirements difficult to meet?
<--- Score

42. How will variation in the actual durations of each activity be dealt with to ensure that the expected ISO 20000 results are met?
<--- Score

43. What are the testing and initial compliance requirements?
<--- Score

44. What is the context?
<--- Score

45. Are roles and responsibilities defined, and where applicable is the appropriate training provided?
<--- Score

46. Are responsibilities and authorities defined?
<--- Score

47. Are the requirements, as captured, unambiguous?
<--- Score

48. What will be required from the business users, in terms of time and effort?
<--- Score

49. How do you keep key subject matter experts in the loop?
<--- Score

50. Are stakeholder processes mapped?
<--- Score

51. How do you manage changes in ISO 20000 requirements?
<--- Score

52. Where can you gather more information?
<--- Score

53. Are customer(s) identified and segmented according to their different needs and requirements?
<--- Score

54. Scope of sensitive information?
<--- Score

55. What critical content must be communicated – who, what, when, where, and how?
<--- Score

56. What was/is the definition of biogas adoption for the program?
<--- Score

57. How does the ISO 20000 manager ensure against scope creep?
<--- Score

58. What awareness and knowledge is required?
<--- Score

59. What are the record-keeping requirements of ISO 20000 activities?
<--- Score

60. Are hosting organizations liable in case of defect of security/software systems?
<--- Score

61. What are the notification, recordkeeping and reporting requirements?
<--- Score

62. Is the physical records management also in scope?
<--- Score

63. Has anyone else (internal or external to the group) attempted to solve this problem or a similar one before? If so, what knowledge can be leveraged from these previous efforts?
<--- Score

64. Are different versions of process maps needed to account for the different types of inputs?
<--- Score

65. Has a team charter been developed and communicated?
<--- Score

66. How do you hand over ISO 20000 context?
<--- Score

67. Is the current 'as is' process being followed? If not, what are the discrepancies?
<--- Score

68. Is the team sponsored by a champion or stakeholder leader?
<--- Score

69. What is the definition of success?
<--- Score

70. How did the ISO 20000 manager receive input to the development of a ISO 20000 improvement plan and the estimated completion dates/times of each activity?
<--- Score

71. Does the policy commit to fulfilling service requirements and include a framework for setting and reviewing service management objectives?
<--- Score

72. Is data collected and displayed to better understand customer(s) critical needs and requirements.
<--- Score

73. What are the requirements for the vendor be able to move workloads to a public/shared cloud?
<--- Score

74. How have you defined all ISO 20000 requirements first?
<--- Score

75. Are approval levels defined for contracts and supplements to contracts?
<--- Score

76. What are the requirements during periods of startup, shutdown, and malfunction?
<--- Score

77. Is there regularly 100% attendance at the team meetings? If not, have appointed substitutes attended to preserve cross-functionality and full representation?
<--- Score

78. Has a high-level 'as is' process map been completed, verified and validated?
<--- Score

79. Do you define SLAs for anything complex?
<--- Score

80. When are meeting minutes sent out? Who is on the distribution list?
<--- Score

81. Do you control changes to service requirements and agreements?
<--- Score

82. How will the ISO 20000 team and the group measure complete success of ISO 20000?
<--- Score

83. Are audit criteria, scope, frequency and methods defined?
<--- Score

84. Is there a completed SIPOC representation, describing the Suppliers, Inputs, Process, Outputs, and Customers?
<--- Score

85. What customer feedback methods were used to solicit their input?

<--- Score

86. What are (control) requirements for ISO 20000 Information?
<--- Score

87. Is ISO 20000 currently on schedule according to the plan?
<--- Score

88. What are the HIPAA requirements?
<--- Score

89. Has top management communicated the importance of fulfilling service, legal and regulatory requirements, and meeting contractual obligations?
<--- Score

90. What are the compelling stakeholder reasons for embarking on ISO 20000?
<--- Score

91. Is there a completed, verified, and validated high-level 'as is' (not 'should be' or 'could be') stakeholder process map?
<--- Score

92. What is the minimum length of time a contingency role will be required for?
<--- Score

93. Should licenses be defined as configuration items?
<--- Score

94. When is/was the ISO 20000 start date?
<--- Score

95. Is there a critical path to deliver ISO 20000 results?
<--- Score

96. Is ISO 20000 linked to key stakeholder goals and objectives?
<--- Score

97. Do you include or refer to the requirements that should be met?
<--- Score

98. What key stakeholder process output measure(s) does ISO 20000 leverage and how?
<--- Score

99. Who are the ISO 20000 improvement team members, including Management Leads and Coaches?
<--- Score

100. Will team members regularly document their ISO 20000 work?
<--- Score

101. Are there different segments of customers?
<--- Score

102. Is full participation by members in regularly held team meetings guaranteed?
<--- Score

103. Is a fully trained team formed, supported, and committed to work on the ISO 20000 improvements?

<--- Score

104. What are the requirements of the ISO 20000?
<--- Score

105. Is the team equipped with available and reliable resources?
<--- Score

106. Is the team formed and are team leaders (Coaches and Management Leads) assigned?
<--- Score

107. What are the Roles and Responsibilities for each team member and its leadership? Where is this documented?
<--- Score

108. Are resources adequate for the scope?
<--- Score

109. What is out-of-scope initially?
<--- Score

110. Is the improvement team aware of the different versions of a process: what they think it is vs. what it actually is vs. what it should be vs. what it could be?
<--- Score

111. What constraints exist that might impact the team?
<--- Score

112. What competences & training are required?
<--- Score

113. Do you all define ISO 20000 in the same way?
<--- Score

114. What are the boundaries of the scope? What is in bounds and what is not? What is the start point? What is the stop point?
<--- Score

115. How often are the team meetings?
<--- Score

116. Has a project plan, Gantt chart, or similar been developed/completed?
<--- Score

117. Is the work to date meeting requirements?
<--- Score

118. Has a ISO 20000 requirement not been met?
<--- Score

119. Is the team adequately staffed with the desired cross-functionality? If not, what additional resources are available to the team?
<--- Score

120. Is there a ISO 20000 management charter, including stakeholder case, problem and goal statements, scope, milestones, roles and responsibilities, communication plan?
<--- Score

121. How is the team tracking and documenting its work?
<--- Score

122. How do you gather ISO 20000 requirements?
<--- Score

123. In what way can you redefine the criteria of choice clients have in your category in your favor?
<--- Score

124. Is the scope of ISO 20000 defined?
<--- Score

125. Is scanning/digitization under scope of the project?
<--- Score

126. What are the rough order estimates on cost savings/opportunities that ISO 20000 brings?
<--- Score

127. What is the scope of the ISO 20000 effort?
<--- Score

128. What are the mandatory requirements and what are the desired requirements?
<--- Score

129. Has the improvement team collected the 'voice of the customer' (obtained feedback – qualitative and quantitative)?
<--- Score

130. Does the team have regular meetings?
<--- Score

131. What are the core elements of the ISO 20000 business case?
<--- Score

132. Is the ISO 20000 scope manageable?
<--- Score

133. Do you ensure that customers agree with your definition?
<--- Score

Add up total points for this section:
_____ = Total points for this section

Divided by: ______ (number of statements answered) = ______ Average score for this section

Transfer your score to the ISO 20000 Index at the beginning of the Self-Assessment.

CRITERION #3: MEASURE:

INTENT: Gather the correct data.
Measure the current performance and
evolution of the situation.

In my belief, the answer to this
question is clearly defined:

5 Strongly Agree

4 Agree

3 Neutral

2 Disagree

1 Strongly Disagree

1. What has the team done to assure the stability and accuracy of the measurement process?
<--- Score

2. How much is software costing us, and what are its benefits?
<--- Score

3. Have you found any 'ground fruit' or 'low-

hanging fruit' for immediate remedies to the gap in performance?
<--- Score

4. What particular quality tools did the team find helpful in establishing measurements?
<--- Score

5. When are costs are incurred?
<--- Score

6. Are actual costs in line with budgeted costs?
<--- Score

7. Do you have a process for analysing power consumption of IT equipment?
<--- Score

8. Was a data collection plan established?
<--- Score

9. What key measures identified indicate the performance of the stakeholder process?
<--- Score

10. How do you verify the ISO 20000 requirements quality?
<--- Score

11. What charts has the team used to display the components of variation in the process?
<--- Score

12. Do you verify that process interfaces are properly defined?
<--- Score

13. What causes innovation to fail or succeed in your organization?
<--- Score

14. Are risks to your organization caused by IT documented?
<--- Score

15. What have been the projects key results outputs, outcomes, and impact, if possible?
<--- Score

16. What are the impacts to your organization?
<--- Score

17. What are the key input variables? What are the key process variables? What are the key output variables?
<--- Score

18. How can you reduce the costs of obtaining inputs?
<--- Score

19. How is the value delivered by ISO 20000 being measured?
<--- Score

20. How large is the gap between current performance and the customer-specified (goal) performance?
<--- Score

21. What are your operating costs?
<--- Score

22. What are the costs and benefits?

<--- Score

23. Are key measures identified and agreed upon?
<--- Score

24. Does management have the right priorities among projects?
<--- Score

25. Do you verify that processes meet your requirements?
<--- Score

26. How do you measure lifecycle phases?
<--- Score

27. What are the ISO 20000 investment costs?
<--- Score

28. Was a business case (cost/benefit) developed?
<--- Score

29. How long to keep data and how to manage retention costs?
<--- Score

30. What is your cost benefit analysis?
<--- Score

31. Have you put appropriate policies and procedures in place to effectively forecast, budget and control your service delivery costs?
<--- Score

32. Do you verify that your service processes are being followed?

<--- Score

33. What is the total cost related to deploying ISO 20000, including any consulting or professional services?
<--- Score

34. Who participated in the data collection for measurements?
<--- Score

35. At what cost?
<--- Score

36. Are the units of measure consistent?
<--- Score

37. What is the total fixed cost?
<--- Score

38. What is the ISO 20000 business impact?
<--- Score

39. Do you analyze your customer satisfaction measurement results?
<--- Score

40. Are high impact defects defined and identified in the stakeholder process?
<--- Score

41. Are control measure already in place?
<--- Score

42. Do you analyse data and trends on incidents and problems to identify the root cause and

possible preventive actions?
<--- Score

43. How do you stay flexible and focused to recognize larger ISO 20000 results?
<--- Score

44. How should costs be charged to the user departments?
<--- Score

45. Is it possible to have an accurate measurement system that is imprecise?
<--- Score

46. What are the agreed upon definitions of the high impact areas, defect(s), unit(s), and opportunities that will figure into the process capability metrics?
<--- Score

47. Do you verify that structures are used to control services?
<--- Score

48. Is long term and short term variability accounted for?
<--- Score

49. How much does it cost?
<--- Score

50. How does an auditor verify that our organization is ISO 20000 compliant?
<--- Score

51. Where is the cost?

<--- Score

52. Is the service being provided at a reasonable cost?
<--- Score

53. What could cause delays in the schedule?
<--- Score

54. Have you made assumptions about the shape of the future, particularly its impact on your customers and competitors?
<--- Score

55. Does your organization systematically track and analyze outcomes related for accountability and quality improvement?
<--- Score

56. Is the cost worth the ISO 20000 effort ?
<--- Score

57. Do you have a change management policy to identify change that could have a major impact on your services or customers?
<--- Score

58. What methods are feasible and acceptable to estimate the impact of reforms?
<--- Score

59. Is a solid data collection plan established that includes measurement systems analysis?
<--- Score

60. What is the root cause(s) of the problem?

<--- Score

61. What is the right balance of time and resources between investigation, analysis, and discussion and dissemination?
<--- Score

62. How do you verify performance?
<--- Score

63. What are your customers expectations and measures?
<--- Score

64. Is Process Variation Displayed/Communicated?
<--- Score

65. What are your key ISO 20000 indicators that you will measure, analyze and track?
<--- Score

66. How will costs be allocated?
<--- Score

67. Do you verify that corrective actions were taken?
<--- Score

68. Is there a Performance Baseline?
<--- Score

69. What are the costs of reform?
<--- Score

70. Is data collected on key measures that were identified?
<--- Score

71. Is key measure data collection planned and executed, process variation displayed and communicated and performance baselined?
<--- Score

72. Which additional factors will impact the customers service quality / performance perception?
<--- Score

73. What data was collected (past, present, future/ ongoing)?
<--- Score

74. What does verifying compliance entail?
<--- Score

75. Is there an opportunity to verify requirements?
<--- Score

76. What users will be impacted?
<--- Score

77. What is the best way to share costs between departments within your organization?
<--- Score

78. Do you review performance to identify causes of nonconformities?
<--- Score

79. How do you verify and develop ideas and innovations?
<--- Score

80. Is data collection planned and executed?
<--- Score

81. Are process variation components displayed/ communicated using suitable charts, graphs, plots?
<--- Score

82. How will effects be measured?
<--- Score

83. Who pays the cost?
<--- Score

84. Will low focus add value to your organization?
<--- Score

85. How can you measure the performance?
<--- Score

86. Do you aggressively reward and promote the people who have the biggest impact on creating excellent ISO 20000 services/products?
<--- Score

87. When is Root Cause Analysis Required?
<--- Score

88. Which stakeholder characteristics are analyzed?
<--- Score

89. What does your operating model cost?
<--- Score

90. What kind of analytics data will be gathered?
<--- Score

91. How do you measure your cybersecurity posture?
<--- Score

92. What relevant entities could be measured?
<--- Score

93. How are implementation risks to be minimised, and what is probability and impact?
<--- Score

94. When a disaster occurs, who gets priority?
<--- Score

95. What is the cost of poor quality software in your organization?
<--- Score

96. What is the lead time and cost for production of the new item?
<--- Score

97. Do you quantify and measure customer focused success?
<--- Score

Add up total points for this section:
_____ = Total points for this section

Divided by: ______ (number of statements answered) = ______
Average score for this section

Transfer your score to the ISO 20000 Index at the beginning of the Self-Assessment.

CRITERION #4: ANALYZE:

INTENT: Analyze causes, assumptions and hypotheses.

In my belief, the answer to this question is clearly defined:

5 Strongly Agree

4 Agree

3 Neutral

2 Disagree

1 Strongly Disagree

1. How do you identify specific ISO 20000 investment opportunities and emerging trends?
<--- Score

2. Do members of staff know and adhere to the documented processes?
<--- Score

3. When should itil processes be implemented?
<--- Score

4. Will the institutional environment maintain project outputs?
<--- Score

5. What ISO 20000 data will be collected?
<--- Score

6. What are the processes for audit reporting and management?
<--- Score

7. Where does each department fit in your organizations overall process flow?
<--- Score

8. What resources are required for the process?
<--- Score

9. What tools were used to generate the list of possible causes?
<--- Score

10. Is the process part of the management review process?
<--- Score

11. Have you established a customer relationship management process?
<--- Score

12. Are the processes linked up by consistent information flows?
<--- Score

13. Who will facilitate the team and process?

<--- Score

14. Has the business purpose of the process been explicitly defined?
<--- Score

15. Are management and process owners informed about residual risks?
<--- Score

16. How can the process be improved?
<--- Score

17. Is there an effective inter relationship between processes?
<--- Score

18. What did the team gain from developing a sub-process map?
<--- Score

19. What data needs to be collected or created by the business processes?
<--- Score

20. How will the data be checked for quality?
<--- Score

21. Do you use a change management process to control changes?
<--- Score

22. What are the key project management processes?
<--- Score

23. Are your outputs consistent?
<--- Score

24. Have you defined accountability and governance for any service management processes, or parts of processes, delivered by other parties?
<--- Score

25. What process improvements will be needed?
<--- Score

26. What documented information is required for the operation and control over the process?
<--- Score

27. Do you clarify interfaces between jointly operated processes?
<--- Score

28. What are the inputs to the process?
<--- Score

29. Are there any specific auditing requirements for organizations hosting and processing EHRs?
<--- Score

30. What requirements must the process management fulfill?
<--- Score

31. How will corresponding data be collected?
<--- Score

32. Will there be a data migration requirement?
<--- Score

33. Are all configuration items defined, uniquely identifiable and recorded in a controlled configuration management database that is periodically audited?
<--- Score

34. What quality tools were used to get through the analyze phase?
<--- Score

35. Have the identified commitments and agreements been addressed in setting up the process?
<--- Score

36. What is the critical use exemption process?
<--- Score

37. Is the relationship between the process and the business goals visible?
<--- Score

38. How many processes are included?
<--- Score

39. What conclusions were drawn from the team's data collection and analysis? How did the team reach these conclusions?
<--- Score

40. What data do you need to collect?
<--- Score

41. What were the crucial 'moments of truth' on the process map?

<--- Score

42. Which processes must be implemented?
<--- Score

43. What data is gathered?
<--- Score

44. Were Pareto charts (or similar) used to portray the 'heavy hitters' (or key sources of variation)?
<--- Score

45. Are adequate resources available for the process?
<--- Score

46. How much work time should be allocated for the process manager role?
<--- Score

47. How many data source and internal portal need to consider for integration?
<--- Score

48. Which interfaces does the change management have with other ITSM processes?
<--- Score

49. Have the process stakeholders and the requirements on the process been identified?
<--- Score

50. What are the processes that do so?
<--- Score

51. What tools were used to narrow the list of possible

causes?
<--- Score

52. Is the suppliers process defined and controlled?
<--- Score

53. What are the primary techniques used to integrate multiple process frameworks?
<--- Score

54. What are budget decision makers key concerns throughout the budget process?
<--- Score

55. What data is currently held and how can it be classified?
<--- Score

56. What qualifications are needed?
<--- Score

57. What are the revised rough estimates of the financial savings/opportunity for ISO 20000 improvements?
<--- Score

58. What was your involvement in the initial implementation of ITSM processes?
<--- Score

59. What methods are used to control and run the process?
<--- Score

60. Does project data provide demographic information?

<--- Score

61. What are the ISO 20000 design outputs?
<--- Score

62. How many labor hours does it take to process each order?
<--- Score

63. Do you use change management process to control changes?
<--- Score

64. How easy are new processes to implement?
<--- Score

65. Do you specify all service and process interdependencies?
<--- Score

66. Do you use service level management process to coordinate change?
<--- Score

67. How do you structure your budget process to minimize conflict and maximize employee engagement?
<--- Score

68. Did your processes, dependent on migrated applications, suffer any changes?
<--- Score

69. Where can you get qualified talent today?
<--- Score

70. Have relevant legal and regulatory process requirements been explicitly identified?
<--- Score

71. Is there a strict change management process?
<--- Score

72. Do you identify performance improvement opportunities?
<--- Score

73. What do you need to qualify?
<--- Score

74. Is the process customer explicitly identified?
<--- Score

75. How do mission and objectives affect the ISO 20000 processes of your organization?
<--- Score

76. What is the difference between material handling robots and processing operations robots?
<--- Score

77. What processes should be taken into account?
<--- Score

78. Is the required ISO 20000 data gathered?
<--- Score

79. Were any designed experiments used to generate additional insight into the data analysis?
<--- Score

80. Identify an operational issue in your organization, for example, could a particular task be done more quickly or more efficiently by ISO 20000?
<--- Score

81. What ISO 20000 data should be managed?
<--- Score

82. Have the process results been explicitly agreed with the customer?
<--- Score

83. How is data used for program management and improvement?
<--- Score

84. What authorities should the process manager have?
<--- Score

85. Where are the servers located, and which legislation applies to the data?
<--- Score

86. Is the process identified and appropriately defined?
<--- Score

87. Has sufficient capacity been built to maintain project outputs?
<--- Score

88. How will the data be stored and maintained?
<--- Score

89. Is there any way to speed up the process?

<--- Score

90. What are your outputs?
<--- Score

91. Does your organization have a data protection officer?
<--- Score

92. When should a process be art not science?
<--- Score

93. Were there any improvement opportunities identified from the process analysis?
<--- Score

94. How long did it take before the initial processes selected where actually being used operationally?
<--- Score

95. Have you established a supplier relationship management process?
<--- Score

96. How many business processes are to be automated via workflows?
<--- Score

97. Do you feedback information about releases and outcomes to your change management and incident and service request processes?
<--- Score

98. Is a flowchart of the process to be audited available?

<--- Score

99. What are the benefits of change management process?
<--- Score

100. Which tasks is assigned to each process manager?
<--- Score

101. Do your employees have the opportunity to do what they do best everyday?
<--- Score

102. Who will gather what data?
<--- Score

103. What are the risks and opportunities for the process?
<--- Score

104. Should you invest in industry-recognized qualifications?
<--- Score

105. What are your best practices for minimizing ISO 20000 project risk, while demonstrating incremental value and quick wins throughout the ISO 20000 project lifecycle?
<--- Score

106. How well does management leverage assets to drive profitability?
<--- Score

107. How much data can be collected in the given

timeframe?
<--- Score

108. What is the cost of poor quality as supported by the team's analysis?
<--- Score

109. Who qualifies to gain access to data?
<--- Score

110. What are the disruptive ISO 20000 technologies that enable your organization to radically change your business processes?
<--- Score

111. What itsm process improvement initiatives based on iso/iec 15504 exist?
<--- Score

112. Is there a need for a specific authorisation or licence to host and process data from EHRs?
<--- Score

113. What methods do you use to gather ISO 20000 data?
<--- Score

114. Think about some of the processes you undertake within your organization, which do you own?
<--- Score

115. How timely was the project in producing outputs and outcomes?
<--- Score

116. What does the data say about the performance of the stakeholder process?
<--- Score

117. Are process results managed adequately?
<--- Score

118. Which minimum requirements must be met in the respective processes?
<--- Score

119. Will the data in the product name remain as originally received from source?
<--- Score

120. Do the processes fulfill the ISO 20000 requirements?
<--- Score

121. What qualifications do ISO 20000 leaders need?
<--- Score

122. How do you measure and model your processes to that end result of customer satisfaction?
<--- Score

123. What is the starting point and process?
<--- Score

124. Which processes were implemented and what determined the choice?
<--- Score

125. What issues should be considered in the continuous process manager meetings?

<--- Score

126. Do you understand your management processes today?
<--- Score

127. What were the financial benefits resulting from any 'ground fruit or low-hanging fruit' (quick fixes)?
<--- Score

128. How will the change process be managed?
<--- Score

129. Are ISO 20000 changes recognized early enough to be approved through the regular process?
<--- Score

130. How many itil processes are currently defined and followed in mdot?
<--- Score

131. What information is introduced into the budget process, and when?
<--- Score

132. What systems/processes must you excel at?
<--- Score

133. Can you add value to the current ISO 20000 decision-making process (largely qualitative) by incorporating uncertainty modeling (more quantitative)?
<--- Score

134. What qualifications and skills do you need?
<--- Score

135. What is your main process or activities?
<--- Score

Add up total points for this section:
_____ = Total points for this section

Divided by: ______ (number of statements answered) = ______ Average score for this section

Transfer your score to the ISO 20000 Index at the beginning of the Self-Assessment.

CRITERION #5: IMPROVE:

INTENT: Develop a practical solution. Innovate, establish and test the solution and to measure the results.

In my belief, the answer to this question is clearly defined:

5 Strongly Agree

4 Agree

3 Neutral

2 Disagree

1 Strongly Disagree

1. Who is involved with workflow mapping?
<--- Score

2. Has the policy been communicated by top management and understood by employees?
<--- Score

3. Does the program define specific business practices that will be evaluated?

<--- Score

4. Is the scope clearly documented?
<--- Score

5. Is there a small-scale pilot for proposed improvement(s)? What conclusions were drawn from the outcomes of a pilot?
<--- Score

6. How is knowledge sharing about risk management improved?
<--- Score

7. Which of risk management course is right for you?
<--- Score

8. Who are the ISO 20000 decision makers?
<--- Score

9. How do you link measurement and risk?
<--- Score

10. Which measures can be taken to mitigate each security risk?
<--- Score

11. Risk events: what are the things that could go wrong?
<--- Score

12. What was/is the expected results of implementing ITIL?
<--- Score

13. Are there any environmental risks that may jeopardize the sustainability of project outcomes?
<--- Score

14. Is pilot data collected and analyzed?
<--- Score

15. Do you have a documented procedure for managing all incidents and service requests?
<--- Score

16. Is the optimal solution selected based on testing and analysis?
<--- Score

17. How will the group know that the solution worked?
<--- Score

18. How is continuous improvement applied to risk management?
<--- Score

19. Do you control changes to documented service requirements?
<--- Score

20. Have you agreed and documented a definition of a major incident where top management must be informed/involved?
<--- Score

21. What alternative responses are available to manage risk?
<--- Score

22. Which service changes should be documented in change records?
<--- Score

23. How can skill-level changes improve ISO 20000?
<--- Score

24. Who are the key stakeholders for the ISO 20000 evaluation?
<--- Score

25. Is supporting ISO 20000 documentation required?
<--- Score

26. How do you improve your likelihood of success ?
<--- Score

27. How do you keep improving ISO 20000?
<--- Score

28. What is the ISO 20000's sustainability risk?
<--- Score

29. Is the project a technically adequate solution to the development problem?
<--- Score

30. Is ISO 20000 documentation maintained?
<--- Score

31. Which of the recognised risks out of all risks can be most likely transferred?
<--- Score

32. Do you promote an understanding of service environment?

<--- Score

33. What can be improved on biogas digester?
<--- Score

34. Can ISO 20000 help you create, deliver, support and improve technology that enables your business?
<--- Score

35. Does ISO 20000 provide a way to measure improvement in the delivery of it service management?
<--- Score

36. Are the key business and technology risks being managed?
<--- Score

37. How do you measure improved ISO 20000 service perception, and satisfaction?
<--- Score

38. Have you developed an approach for managing information security incidents and risks, and implemented appropriate controls?
<--- Score

39. Are risk triggers captured?
<--- Score

40. Do you add value or assume risk?
<--- Score

41. Does the present ITIL version provide effective mechanisms for risk management?

<--- Score

42. Is there any other ISO 20000 solution?
<--- Score

43. Are procedures documented for managing ISO 20000 risks?
<--- Score

44. What tools were used to tap into the creativity and encourage 'outside the box' thinking?
<--- Score

45. Do you promote an understanding of business environment?
<--- Score

46. What attendant changes will need to be made to ensure that the solution is successful?
<--- Score

47. How does the solution remove the key sources of issues discovered in the analyze phase?
<--- Score

48. How do you mitigate ISO 20000 risk?
<--- Score

49. Has top management ensured that risks to services are identified, assessed and managed?
<--- Score

50. What can be done to improve its effectiveness, that is, how can IT management be proactive and help organizations respond to business change more effectively?

<--- Score

51. Who manages supplier risk management in your organization?
<--- Score

52. Is there a cost/benefit analysis of optimal solution(s)?
<--- Score

53. How do you define the solutions' scope?
<--- Score

54. What assumptions are made about the solution and approach?
<--- Score

55. What current systems have to be understood and/or changed?
<--- Score

56. How do you manage ISO 20000 risk?
<--- Score

57. Are you tired and frustrated with chasing approvers on simple, low risk frequent changes?
<--- Score

58. When is risk assessment performed?
<--- Score

59. Did you document your complaint management procedure?
<--- Score

60. Is the implementation plan designed?

<--- Score

61. Is the solution technically practical?
<--- Score

62. Was a pilot designed for the proposed solution(s)?
<--- Score

63. What error proofing will be done to address some of the discrepancies observed in the 'as is' process?
<--- Score

64. Did you develop a service complaint management procedure?
<--- Score

65. To what extent does management recognize ISO 20000 as a tool to increase the results?
<--- Score

66. What tools were most useful during the improve phase?
<--- Score

67. When you map the key players in your own work and the types/domains of relationships with them, which relationships do you find easy and which challenging, and why?
<--- Score

68. What is the implementation plan?
<--- Score

69. Has your organization mapped its internal and external stakeholders?
<--- Score

70. What do departments find to be the major obstacles in policy formation and policy decision?
<--- Score

71. What will an artificial mind that has reached the human level of reasoning decide to do next?
<--- Score

72. What are the risks involved in the change?
<--- Score

73. Is the ISO 20000 solution sustainable?
<--- Score

74. Who controls key decisions that will be made?
<--- Score

75. What does the 'should be' process map/design look like?
<--- Score

76. Has the access speed to the applications has been improved?
<--- Score

77. Do you have a documented procedure to record, track and control versions of configuration items to ensure integrity?
<--- Score

78. Which are realistic, feasible, and helpful in the roadmap timeline?
<--- Score

79. How can you improve performance?

<--- Score

80. What are the ISO 20000 security risks?
<--- Score

81. How are policy decisions made and where?
<--- Score

82. Will adoption of cloud computing put the enterprise at risk?
<--- Score

83. Why implement risk based thinking?
<--- Score

84. What are the measurable short term and longer term results the project will achieve?
<--- Score

85. What is ISO 20000 risk?
<--- Score

86. If you could go back in time five years, what decision would you make differently? What is your best guess as to what decision you're making today you might regret five years from now?
<--- Score

87. How are risks recognized, evaluated and mitigated currently?
<--- Score

88. What lessons, if any, from a pilot were incorporated into the design of the full-scale solution?
<--- Score

89. What is the quality of the results?
<--- Score

90. What were the underlying assumptions on the cost-benefit analysis?
<--- Score

91. What communications are necessary to support the implementation of the solution?
<--- Score

92. Can the solution be designed and implemented within an acceptable time period?
<--- Score

93. How does your organization determine the optimum delivery strategy?
<--- Score

94. What needs improvement? Why?
<--- Score

95. What criteria will you use to assess your ISO 20000 risks?
<--- Score

96. How do you benefit from the environmental risk assessment?
<--- Score

97. Have you agreed and documented a definition and approach to managing emergency change with the customer?
<--- Score

98. Is a solution implementation plan established,

including schedule/work breakdown structure, resources, risk management plan, cost/budget, and control plan?
<--- Score

99. Are risk management tasks balanced centrally and locally?
<--- Score

100. What are the affordable ISO 20000 risks?
<--- Score

101. Do you document the relationship suppliers have with suppliers?
<--- Score

102. Will the controls trigger any other risks?
<--- Score

103. Risk Identification: What are the possible risk events your organization faces in relation to ISO 20000?
<--- Score

104. What tools were used to evaluate the potential solutions?
<--- Score

105. Who manages ISO 20000 risk?
<--- Score

106. How do you handle risk assessing your clients information assets?
<--- Score

107. What should the implementing organizations

understand and do?
<--- Score

108. Can you integrate quality management and risk management?
<--- Score

109. What are the concrete ISO 20000 results?
<--- Score

110. Do you document customers, users, and related interested parties?
<--- Score

111. Who are the ISO 20000 decision-makers?
<--- Score

112. Is a contingency plan established?
<--- Score

113. Are the most efficient solutions problem-specific?
<--- Score

114. Has an independent biogas digester market resulted from the program?
<--- Score

115. What is the team's contingency plan for potential problems occurring in implementation?
<--- Score

116. Do you record the results of supplier performance measurements?
<--- Score

117. Are the risks fully understood, reasonable and

manageable?
<--- Score

118. How will the team or the process owner(s) monitor the implementation plan to see that it is working as intended?
<--- Score

119. What is ISO 20000's impact on utilizing the best solution(s)?
<--- Score

120. Does your organization identify and assess potential environmental risks?
<--- Score

121. Were any criteria developed to assist the team in testing and evaluating potential solutions?
<--- Score

122. Do you have the optimal project management team structure?
<--- Score

123. Is risk periodically assessed?
<--- Score

124. Is it possible that a similar structure exists among different decisionmaking systems?
<--- Score

125. Have you assessed and documented the risks to service continuity and availability, including customer requirements?
<--- Score

126. How did the team generate the list of possible solutions?
<--- Score

127. Is it acceptable to put your business at risk in the name of ethics?
<--- Score

128. When implementing itil in your organization, how do you implement risk management?
<--- Score

129. What are the main issues leading to software development team dissatisfaction?
<--- Score

130. What tools do you use once you have decided on a ISO 20000 strategy and more importantly how do you choose?
<--- Score

Add up total points for this section:
_____ = Total points for this section

Divided by: ______ (number of statements answered) = ______
Average score for this section

Transfer your score to the ISO 20000 Index at the beginning of the Self-Assessment.

CRITERION #6: CONTROL:

INTENT: Implement the practical solution. Maintain the performance and correct possible complications.

In my belief, the answer to this question is clearly defined:

5 Strongly Agree

4 Agree

3 Neutral

2 Disagree

1 Strongly Disagree

1. Will the true service management plan rise?
<--- Score

2. Are documented procedures clear and easy to follow for the operators?
<--- Score

3. What could a project plan for ISO 20000 look like?

<--- Score

4. Are suggested corrective/restorative actions indicated on the response plan for known causes to problems that might surface?
<--- Score

5. What does your organization/do you need to be able to scale up operations and reach more clients?
<--- Score

6. Will any special training be provided for results interpretation?
<--- Score

7. How can financial management provide visibility and control over value creation?
<--- Score

8. How might the group capture best practices and lessons learned so as to leverage improvements?
<--- Score

9. Who is the ISO 20000 process owner?
<--- Score

10. Can support from partners be adjusted?
<--- Score

11. Will your goals reflect your program budget?
<--- Score

12. Is the workforce center using the strategic plan to offer training?
<--- Score

13. How do you plan for the cost of succession?
<--- Score

14. Do you verify that contracts reflect current requirements?
<--- Score

15. What drives the quality of certifiable management system standards implementation?
<--- Score

16. How will the process owner verify improvement in present and future sigma levels, process capabilities?
<--- Score

17. Which processes where planned for future phases?
<--- Score

18. What characteristic do the ISO/IEC 27001 and ISO/IEC 20000 standards have in common?
<--- Score

19. How will the process owner and team be able to hold the gains?
<--- Score

20. Does job training on the documented procedures need to be part of the process team's education and training?
<--- Score

21. Is the knowledge you have learned visible to others?
<--- Score

22. What do you consider a successful standard?
<--- Score

23. Do you have a capacity plan in place that considers the human, technical, information and financial resources required to meet agreed capacity and performance requirements?
<--- Score

24. Why does unsupervised pre training help deep learning?
<--- Score

25. Which is the true service management plan?
<--- Score

26. Do you have reports in place to review the performance of your services against agreed targets?
<--- Score

27. Do you measure performance against contractual obligations?
<--- Score

28. What is the relationship between learning strategies and academic performance?
<--- Score

29. Do you have a plan to effectively and efficiently remove services where appropriate?
<--- Score

30. Are new process steps, standards, and documentation ingrained into normal operations?

<--- Score

31. Is the market really aware of the ITIL framework and the ISO 20000 standard?
<--- Score

32. Do you monitor the effectiveness of your ISO 20000 activities?
<--- Score

33. Is there a transfer of ownership and knowledge to process owner and process team tasked with the responsibilities.
<--- Score

34. Are the planned controls working?
<--- Score

35. Is a response plan established and deployed?
<--- Score

36. Do you monitor the performance of suppliers at planned intervals?
<--- Score

37. How will input, process, and output variables be checked to detect for sub-optimal conditions?
<--- Score

38. Where do you learn more about GDPR?
<--- Score

39. Do you review your service performance at planned intervals?
<--- Score

40. Implementation Planning: is a pilot needed to test the changes before a full roll out occurs?
<--- Score

41. What are customers monitoring?
<--- Score

42. Is there a plan to ensure you evaluate and report on the new or changed service performance against expected outcomes?
<--- Score

43. What ISO 20000 standards are applicable?
<--- Score

44. Is there a ISO 20000 Communication plan covering who needs to get what information when?
<--- Score

45. What is the recommended frequency of auditing?
<--- Score

46. What quality tools were useful in the control phase?
<--- Score

47. Has your organization developed privacy/data protection related standards?
<--- Score

48. Is a response plan in place for when the input, process, or output measures indicate an 'out-of-control' condition?
<--- Score

49. Are there any specific rules/standards on the

interoperability of EHR?
<--- Score

50. Is there a control plan in place for sustaining improvements (short and long-term)?
<--- Score

51. Are there requirements of standards the service provider needs to abide by?
<--- Score

52. Is there a recommended audit plan for routine surveillance inspections of ISO 20000's gains?
<--- Score

53. What are your results for key measures or indicators of the accomplishment of your ISO 20000 strategy and action plans, including building and strengthening core competencies?
<--- Score

54. Will existing staff require re-training, for example, to learn new business processes?
<--- Score

55. Is implementing multiple management system standards a hindrance to innovation?
<--- Score

56. Can the current standards and models serve as a reference?
<--- Score

57. Against what alternative is success being measured?
<--- Score

58. What is the control/monitoring plan?
<--- Score

59. Are private labor standard a complement or a substitute to traditional labor regulations?
<--- Score

60. How do you select, collect, align, and integrate ISO 20000 data and information for tracking daily operations and overall organizational performance, including progress relative to strategic objectives and action plans?
<--- Score

61. Has a service management plan been created, implemented and maintained in line with the policy, objectives and service requirements?
<--- Score

62. Do you have a process to plan, design and develop, test and transition new or changed services into the live environment?
<--- Score

63. Is there any guidance on when entities will be expected to have the plan fully implemented?
<--- Score

64. How each segment could benefit from various international standards?
<--- Score

65. Do you measure customer satisfaction at planned intervals?
<--- Score

66. Will cloud computing change standards in it service management?
<--- Score

67. In the case of a ISO 20000 project, the criteria for the audit derive from implementation objectives, an audit of a ISO 20000 project involves assessing whether the recommendations outlined for implementation have been met, can you track that any ISO 20000 project is implemented as planned, and is it working?
<--- Score

68. Is there a standardized process?
<--- Score

69. How do you go about planning and performing an ISMS internal audit?
<--- Score

70. Are there documented procedures?
<--- Score

71. Does the ISO 20000 performance meet the customer's requirements?
<--- Score

72. Is reporting being used or needed?
<--- Score

73. Do you analyse change requests at planned intervals to identify trends and opportunities for improvement?
<--- Score

74. What is according to ISO/IEC 20000 a required part of the planning for new or changed services?
<--- Score

75. What kind of organizations can benefit from the standard?
<--- Score

76. How does self regulated learning relate to active procrastination and other learning behaviors?
<--- Score

77. Has top management committed to conducting management reviews at planned intervals?
<--- Score

78. Do you measure supplier performance against service targets?
<--- Score

79. Does the product conform to international standards?
<--- Score

80. What emission limits and work practice standards must you meet?
<--- Score

81. Why revise the standard and what are the differences?
<--- Score

82. Is there a documented and implemented monitoring plan?

<--- Score

83. Has the improved process and its steps been standardized?
<--- Score

84. Which ITSM standards / frameworks / methodologies do your it department use?
<--- Score

85. Did things happen according to plan?
<--- Score

86. How easy was the user interface to learn?
<--- Score

87. Will the team be available to assist members in planning investigations?
<--- Score

88. Is knowledge gained on process shared and institutionalized?
<--- Score

89. Act/Adjust: What Do you Need to Do Differently?
<--- Score

90. Do the viable solutions scale to future needs?
<--- Score

91. How will new or emerging customer needs/ requirements be checked/communicated to orient the process toward meeting the new specifications and continually reducing variation?
<--- Score

92. What are the key elements of your ISO 20000 performance improvement system, including your evaluation, organizational learning, and innovation processes?
<--- Score

93. How will the day-to-day responsibilities for monitoring and continual improvement be transferred from the improvement team to the process owner?
<--- Score

94. Does the response plan contain a definite closed loop continual improvement scheme (e.g., plan-do-check-act)?
<--- Score

95. What are the critical parameters to watch?
<--- Score

96. Have new or revised work instructions resulted?
<--- Score

97. Are learning strategies malleable?
<--- Score

98. Who monitors and measures the process?
<--- Score

99. How will report readings be checked to effectively monitor performance?
<--- Score

100. What key inputs and outputs are being measured on an ongoing basis?
<--- Score

101. Does ISO 20000 appropriately measure and monitor risk?
<--- Score

102. What purpose can the ISO/IEC 20000 standard serve?
<--- Score

103. Will a program or service benefit from economies of scale?
<--- Score

104. Are operating procedures consistent?
<--- Score

105. Is process performance planned and monitored adequately?
<--- Score

106. Is new knowledge gained imbedded in the response plan?
<--- Score

107. What are the reasons for updating standards in the field of privacy/data protection?
<--- Score

108. Is real time monitoring needed or practical for responsive load?
<--- Score

109. Have all test plans been completed successfully?
<--- Score

110. Is there documentation that will support the successful operation of the improvement?
<--- Score

111. Does a troubleshooting guide exist or is it needed?
<--- Score

112. What other systems, operations, processes, and infrastructures (hiring practices, staffing, training, incentives/rewards, metrics/dashboards/scorecards, etc.) need updates, additions, changes, or deletions in order to facilitate knowledge transfer and improvements?
<--- Score

113. Is the performance of your service management activity being monitored and reported on as outlined in the plan?
<--- Score

114. What adjustments to the strategies are needed?
<--- Score

115. Do the ISO 20000 decisions you make today help people and the planet tomorrow?
<--- Score

116. What should the next improvement project be that is related to ISO 20000?
<--- Score

117. How often do you use digital learning arrangements in your instruction?
<--- Score

118. What are the backup software, backup monitoring tool and media currently used?
<--- Score

119. Do you review the performance of your service with the customer at planned intervals?
<--- Score

120. What other areas of the group might benefit from the ISO 20000 team's improvements, knowledge, and learning?
<--- Score

121. Has a documented procedure been produced for planning, conducting and reporting on internal audits?
<--- Score

122. How do your controls stack up?
<--- Score

123. Is the release compatible with the software release plan?
<--- Score

124. What are the infrastructure monitoring and management tools that are used?
<--- Score

125. Where is the accountability in international accountability standards?
<--- Score

126. What frameworks/standards is your organization using?
<--- Score

127. Why do other organizations standardize?
<--- Score

128. Are there requirements of other standards the service provider needs to abide by?
<--- Score

Add up total points for this section:
_____ = Total points for this section

Divided by: ______ (number of statements answered) = ______ Average score for this section

Transfer your score to the ISO 20000 Index at the beginning of the Self-Assessment.

CRITERION #7: SUSTAIN:

INTENT: Retain the benefits.

In my belief, the answer to this question is clearly defined:

5 Strongly Agree

4 Agree

3 Neutral

2 Disagree

1 Strongly Disagree

1. Are you receiving adequate IT services and value for money from your IT services suppliers?
<--- Score

2. How many biogas digester have you financed in the last year?
<--- Score

3. Which machine organization should buy?
<--- Score

4. How do you benefit from accident investigation?
<--- Score

5. What is the preferred mode of project execution?
<--- Score

6. Are all key stakeholders present at all Structured Walkthroughs?
<--- Score

7. Do you manage your relationship with your suppliers suppliers?
<--- Score

8. Did your organization deliver a good or service?
<--- Score

9. What type and size of biogas digester do you own?
<--- Score

10. How are ancillary services characterized?
<--- Score

11. Does cloud computing deliver the promised benefits for IT industry?
<--- Score

12. How do you expect to effectively manage the business tomorrow, or even worse get someone else to manage it?
<--- Score

13. What is the estimated work effort for upgrade activities?

<--- Score

14. What disadvantages do you see from implementing your model?
<--- Score

15. Why is ISO 20000 important for your business?
<--- Score

16. How do you keep records, of what?
<--- Score

17. How many it and/or information security professionals do you currently employ?
<--- Score

18. Do you assign responsibility for managing supplier performance?
<--- Score

19. What is a purpose of ISO/IEC 20000?
<--- Score

20. How could the roles be implemented in the best possible manner?
<--- Score

21. Should we pause and look at ISO 20000 as we move forward?
<--- Score

22. Are information systems managers ready?
<--- Score

23. Do you use your procedure to manage customer complaints?

<--- Score

24. How many maximum users anticipated through out all your organizations?
<--- Score

25. What is value from a customer perspective?
<--- Score

26. How can confidentiality of information be attained?
<--- Score

27. Are there parts of the ISMS that are self evidently painful to operate?
<--- Score

28. Do you include or refer to how service contracts can be changed?
<--- Score

29. Do you include or refer to service levels that suppliers must maintain?
<--- Score

30. What is the added value of a service being delivered?
<--- Score

31. Why is regulation always the highest priced ancillary service?
<--- Score

32. Did your organization receive a payment?
<--- Score

33. Are you a manager with an interest in the long term success of your business?
<--- Score

34. Are the procedures being implemented and maintained?
<--- Score

35. How do enterprise design patterns relate to the enterprise?
<--- Score

36. What is the key purpose of the service?
<--- Score

37. Does the project have an exit strategy?
<--- Score

38. What is the minimum available level of functionality of the service?
<--- Score

39. What are the benefits and drawbacks of the ITIL / ISO 20000 framework?
<--- Score

40. Do you include or refer to how services can be terminated?
<--- Score

41. Are there different archiving rules for different providers and organizations?
<--- Score

42. What percentage of earned revenue is from your organizations core programs and services?

<--- Score

43. What contribution has the program made to your biogas digester?
<--- Score

44. Is anybody working with ITIL or ISO 20000?
<--- Score

45. Are attendance sheets available for review on all projects?
<--- Score

46. What can be done to make the project more effective?
<--- Score

47. Did your organization make a payment?
<--- Score

48. How is debt service coverage ratio calculated?
<--- Score

49. Do you clarify how service complaints are investigated?
<--- Score

50. When information truly is ubiquitous, when reach and connectivity are completely global, when computing resources are infinite, and when a whole new set of impossibilities are not only possible, but happening, what will that do to your business?
<--- Score

51. How many biogas units have you installed during the last year?

<--- Score

52. Are you still engaged in biogas production?
<--- Score

53. Who are your customers?
<--- Score

54. What are your personal philosophies regarding ISO 20000 and how do they influence your work?
<--- Score

55. Did your organization your organizations revenues exceed its expenses?
<--- Score

56. Is it possible to solve the incident with a service request?
<--- Score

57. What features of project management enabled efficiency?
<--- Score

58. Is it economical; do you have the time and money?
<--- Score

59. Why technology in your business?
<--- Score

60. Do you clarify how service complaints are acted upon?
<--- Score

61. How much time is spent on invoicing?
<--- Score

62. Have the objectives during the implementation of the biogas program changed and if so, why and how?
<--- Score

63. Where do the supervisors spend time?
<--- Score

64. What could be benefits of ISO 20000?
<--- Score

65. Do you designate a relationship manager for each customer?
<--- Score

66. What is accreditatio io the ciotext if ISO/IEC 20000?
<--- Score

67. Are there any companies that cannot be certified according to ISO 20000?
<--- Score

68. What is ISO/IEC 20000 it service management?
<--- Score

69. What is the purpose of ISO 20000 in relation to the mission?
<--- Score

70. Do kpis used by cios decelerate digital business transformation?
<--- Score

71. Is there any relationship between safety

metrics and software metrics?
<--- Score

72. What are the key benefits to your business?
<--- Score

73. What can be done by other partner to increase uptake of finance for biogas?
<--- Score

74. What types of releases exist in your organization?
<--- Score

75. What price should you set for a new fee based service?
<--- Score

76. How changes are approved for implementation?
<--- Score

77. What projects are going on in the organization today, and what resources are those projects using from the resource pools?
<--- Score

78. How do you capture value for your stakeholders?
<--- Score

79. How long will it take to change?
<--- Score

80. What made you aim for more with ISO 20000?
<--- Score

81. What percentage of your information security budget is currently spent on personnel and training?
<--- Score

82. What is new about cloud computing security?
<--- Score

83. Are the code blocks reviewed that are selected by the project design team?
<--- Score

84. Does your organization have non current liabilities?
<--- Score

85. What are the components of ISO/IEC 20000?
<--- Score

86. Does the service meet the expectations agreed upon?
<--- Score

87. What exactly does ISO 20000 reveal?
<--- Score

88. Do you have what it takes to achieve cybersecurity excellence in your organization?
<--- Score

89. How many organizations have been assessed or certified under the program?
<--- Score

90. Who is likely to benefit most from an objective?

<--- Score

91. Have appropriate software licences been purchased or reallocated licences used?
<--- Score

92. Should it services be provided internally or externally, and how does that affect the big picture?
<--- Score

93. Has it received a good or service?
<--- Score

94. Who will determine interim and final deadlines?
<--- Score

95. What were your initial expectations, before the biogas digester was installed?
<--- Score

96. How do you enhance employee performance?
<--- Score

97. What is the relationship between its current and non current assets?
<--- Score

98. What can be done to increase the number biogas units financed by your institution?
<--- Score

99. What happens if the office manager makes copies?
<--- Score

100. Do you assign responsibility for managing supplier relationships?
<--- Score

101. Can itil really work in an outsourced environment?
<--- Score

102. Is the ISO 20000 organization completing tasks effectively and efficiently?
<--- Score

103. How valuable is information and communication technology?
<--- Score

104. Do you provide it services that meet increasing business demands for continuous operation?
<--- Score

105. What is business relationship management?
<--- Score

106. How far has the project achieved its overall objectives?
<--- Score

107. How many companies and/or organizations have adopted the quality program?
<--- Score

108. What can/should the program do differently to enhance adoption of biogas in your area?
<--- Score

109. Do you clarify how service complaints are reported?
<--- Score

110. How do you spread information?
<--- Score

111. Did your organization receive a good or service?
<--- Score

112. Which roles are related to change management?
<--- Score

113. Should every change implementation be treated as a release?
<--- Score

114. How does it apply to cloud computing?
<--- Score

115. Is ISO 14001 a gateway to more advanced voluntary action?
<--- Score

116. Are you familiar with ITIL / ISO 20000?
<--- Score

117. Do you consider your service performance with customers?
<--- Score

118. What is meant by highest quality?
<--- Score

119. How useful is executive function training?
<--- Score

120. In a project to restructure ISO 20000 outcomes, which stakeholders would you involve?
<--- Score

121. Why introduce charging for it services?
<--- Score

122. How do you report your training?
<--- Score

123. What do you do for your organization?
<--- Score

124. How good does your organization have to be?
<--- Score

125. Does your organization have the capacity to promote and increase uptake of biogas finance without the intervention of the program?
<--- Score

126. What services should you offer and to whom?
<--- Score

127. Are service level/performance warranties covered in the master service agreement?
<--- Score

128. Can you maintain your growth without detracting from the factors that have contributed to your success?
<--- Score

129. Is the service safe and privacy protected?
<--- Score

130. What is the change attributable to the project?
<--- Score

131. Are there dependencies on other organizations?
<--- Score

132. Who will be responsible for deciding whether ISO 20000 goes ahead or not after the initial investigations?
<--- Score

133. Where can you break convention?
<--- Score

134. Do you have an information security policy?
<--- Score

135. Are there any services that will overlap or compete with any other of the existing services contracts?
<--- Score

136. What are your experiences from using ITIL / ISO 20000?
<--- Score

137. Have appropriate business managers signed off acceptance of the new service?
<--- Score

138. What is service management system and how

it can be managed?
<--- Score

139. Is self service always appropriate?
<--- Score

140. How many reports and what type of reports are to be generated by the system?
<--- Score

141. How do itam teams demonstrate and promote the value?
<--- Score

142. Do you clarify how customer service complaints are handled?
<--- Score

143. How will the IT service provider communicate the benefits of ISO/IEC 20000 to the organization?
<--- Score

144. What were the major reasons for adopting the biogas technology?
<--- Score

145. How likely is it that you would recommend your organization as a good place to work?
<--- Score

146. Do you include or refer to organizational interdependencies?
<--- Score

147. What is the lead time for procuring the new item?

<--- Score

148. Are abandons included in your service level denominator?
<--- Score

149. What benefits does the new version bring?
<--- Score

150. How your organization can become ISO/IEC 20000 certified?
<--- Score

151. Are the assumptions believable and achievable?
<--- Score

152. How successful do you consider the implementation?
<--- Score

153. What is the total amount of storage in the environment per tier or per technology as applicable?
<--- Score

154. What difference has the project made to the beneficiaries?
<--- Score

155. What makes information truly valuable?
<--- Score

156. Do you clarify how service complaints are closed?
<--- Score

157. How do partners demonstrate value?
<--- Score

158. Is maximizing ISO 20000 protection the same as minimizing ISO 20000 loss?
<--- Score

159. Can the partner continue to report on behalf of your organization?
<--- Score

160. Have you implemented a biogas program before?
<--- Score

161. What is project implementation time line?
<--- Score

162. What do you as financial organization do to contribute to biogas digester promotion?
<--- Score

163. Did the report present an assessment of relevant outcomes and achievement of project objectives?
<--- Score

164. Why organizations fail to pass an audit?
<--- Score

165. What is an important concern for the customer in multi tenant environments?
<--- Score

166. What is the customer expectation of the service provided?

<--- Score

167. Who participates in the program?
<--- Score

168. What is an unauthorized commitment?
<--- Score

169. How are ISO 20000 and itil correlated?
<--- Score

170. What about the intelligent hardware and software?
<--- Score

171. Operational - will it work?
<--- Score

172. Do you use representative samples of your customers and users?
<--- Score

173. Will related incident be solved on time?
<--- Score

174. How are self service methods used in the service desk?
<--- Score

175. Why implement it service management?
<--- Score

176. Does every customer have a designated individual who is responsible for managing the customer relationship and satisfaction?
<--- Score

177. What is a benefit to an organization when the services are delivered according to ISO/IEC 20000?
<--- Score

178. What is your experience in/with biogas?
<--- Score

179. Which service model allows the customer to choose more layers in the computing architecture?
<--- Score

180. How can a non incumbent contractor know the number and availability of personnel and have a fixed price rate for work that is so inherently vague?
<--- Score

181. How are ancillary services valued and what are the prices?
<--- Score

182. Do your organizations revenues cover its operating expenses?
<--- Score

183. What is the difference between IaaS and the domain specific services?
<--- Score

184. Which machine would you recommend your organization to buy?
<--- Score

185. What does your signature ensure?
<--- Score

186. How do you provide a safe environment -physically and emotionally?
<--- Score

187. How do you engage the workforce, in addition to satisfying them?
<--- Score

188. How do you benefit from environmental emergency preparedness and response?
<--- Score

189. How does cloud computing change the relationship between provider and customer?
<--- Score

190. Do customer overrides and voluntary response reduce the reliability value of load response?
<--- Score

191. Are you using any tools to implement ITIL?
<--- Score

192. Why is service continuity so important?
<--- Score

193. Do you consider the project outcome of a deployment project as a release?
<--- Score

194. What is the source of the strategies for ISO 20000 strengthening and reform?
<--- Score

195. What is your experience in financing biogas digester?
<--- Score

196. Which reliability services might responsive loads provide?
<--- Score

197. Who owns the service on the customer side?
<--- Score

198. How does ISO 20000 affect your ITIL-based organization?
<--- Score

199. Are you making progress, and are you making progress as ISO 20000 leaders?
<--- Score

200. What are the objectives of the biogas program?
<--- Score

201. Do you clarify how service complaints are escalated?
<--- Score

202. Why you often miss a similar step while exploring important knowledge resources?
<--- Score

203. How can itil and agile project management coexist?
<--- Score

204. What is the tool used for inventory and spares

management?
<--- Score

205. What are the current ITIL aligned services being delivered?
<--- Score

206. How does it affect cloud computing?
<--- Score

207. Is the applied project approach sound and appropriate?
<--- Score

208. What benefits do we expect from ISO/IEC 20000?
<--- Score

209. What threats are the system exposed?
<--- Score

210. How/by whom was biogas first introduced to you?
<--- Score

211. Do you manage your relationship with lead service suppliers?
<--- Score

212. Will the incident be solved on time?
<--- Score

213. What did you expect from the partnership?
<--- Score

214. How well has the project performed?

<--- Score

215. Where is debt service/lease purchase information?
<--- Score

216. Will using responsive loads hurt power system stability?
<--- Score

217. Do you maintain a service catalog that your end users can browse?
<--- Score

218. Do you assign responsibility for managing customer relationships?
<--- Score

219. Is the management really committed?
<--- Score

220. Did you already mention it is a conflict of interest for the same person to implement and audit the system?
<--- Score

221. What level of maturity is evident?
<--- Score

222. Have features been disabled in your organization?
<--- Score

223. Which business interruption do other organizations fear most?
<--- Score

224. What happened to the ISO 9000 lustre?
<--- Score

225. Do you automate through the service management tool?
<--- Score

226. What exactly does ISO certified imply about your organization and what are the benefits?
<--- Score

227. How is ISO 9001 useful to small businesses?
<--- Score

228. What is the relationship between academic perseverance and academic performance?
<--- Score

229. What is your organizations basis of budgeting?
<--- Score

230. How likely is it that the service will work as expected?
<--- Score

231. Who is responsible for the build, test, and implementation of the change?
<--- Score

232. How do you respond to existing and new management challenges?
<--- Score

233. What were/are the objectives of the biogas

program?
<--- Score

234. What is ISO 20000 and how can it help you manage your it services?
<--- Score

235. Do you assign responsibility for managing customer satisfaction?
<--- Score

236. Do you have a flow diagram of what happens?
<--- Score

237. How do you start the implementation from your organizational point of view?
<--- Score

238. Do you maintain a service catalogue that your end users can browse?
<--- Score

239. Do you make extensive use of the information stored in the CMDB?
<--- Score

240. Should system operators encourage and facilitate load response?
<--- Score

241. Are there typical pitfalls in an ISO 20000 project?
<--- Score

242. How do you create buy-in?
<--- Score

243. Does the service provider have contractual obligations to adhere to?
<--- Score

244. What is the potential harm to your information assets?
<--- Score

245. What is your formula for success in ISO 20000 ?
<--- Score

246. Are you maintaining a past–present–future perspective throughout the ISO 20000 discussion?
<--- Score

247. Can your organization continue to report on behalf of the partner?
<--- Score

248. How much are the total benefits of the program?
<--- Score

249. Where is personnel and FTE information?
<--- Score

250. How can you prepare for ISO 20000?
<--- Score

251. Do you align supplier service levels with customer service levels?
<--- Score

252. Did project objectives and interventions remain relevant to beneficiaries?

<--- Score

253. If you do not follow, then how to lead?
<--- Score

254. Is there sufficient public/stakeholder awareness in support of the projects long term objectives?
<--- Score

255. What new services of functionality will be implemented next with ISO 20000 ?
<--- Score

256. How do you efficiently allocate resources across a portfolio of services?
<--- Score

257. What are your most important goals for the strategic ISO 20000 objectives?
<--- Score

258. Is ISO/IEC 20000 intended for individuals or organisations?
<--- Score

259. If you had to rebuild your organization without any traditional competitive advantages (i.e., no killer technology, promising research, innovative product/ service delivery model, etcetera), how would your people have to approach their work and collaborate together in order to create the necessary conditions for success?
<--- Score

260. What are the benefits of being certified?

<--- Score

261. What is configuration management?
<--- Score

262. Is tata communications HIPAA compliant?
<--- Score

263. What happens before a project starts?
<--- Score

264. Have all security checks and tests been completed successfully?
<--- Score

265. Are service levels covered in the master service agreement?
<--- Score

266. What is the kind of project structure that would be appropriate for your ISO 20000 project, should it be formal and complex, or can it be less formal and relatively simple?
<--- Score

267. Why service continuity management?
<--- Score

268. What does ISO 20000 actually look like?
<--- Score

269. How has the service management industry changed in recent years?
<--- Score

270. What does service manager offer?

<--- Score

271. What could ISO have done for you?
<--- Score

272. Who uses your product in ways you never expected?
<--- Score

273. When was the biogas digester installed?
<--- Score

274. How is the research coverage of knowledge areas distributed?
<--- Score

275. Do you create a communication mechanism for each customer?
<--- Score

276. What are the average salaries of your information security professional positions?
<--- Score

277. What better time to call on a few local experts to update your look?
<--- Score

278. Why, in fact, in democratic systems has there been so little demand for income redistribution?
<--- Score

279. What are the reasons for the achievement/ non achievement of the project objectives?
<--- Score

280. What service level in which area?
<--- Score

281. Do you align your supplier service levels with your SLAs?
<--- Score

282. How is input provided to management review?
<--- Score

283. What reference framework could you use with appraising Information Security?
<--- Score

284. Who actually benefits, what groups?
<--- Score

285. How small and medium enterprises can begin the implementation of ITIL?
<--- Score

286. Do you count on the provider organization?
<--- Score

287. Who starts new your organization?
<--- Score

288. Do you clarify how service complaints are recorded?
<--- Score

289. Does the policy relating to ethics, bribery and corruption cover only your organization?
<--- Score

290. What advantages do you see from implementing your model?
<--- Score

291. How well did your organization perform?
<--- Score

292. What could happen if you do not do it?
<--- Score

293. Is it critical to the success of your business?
<--- Score

294. Are any wireless security tools currently in place?
<--- Score

295. What is the current network management platform?
<--- Score

296. How does ISO/IEC 20000 relate to itil?
<--- Score

297. What would be a good reason for organizations to adopt ISO/IEC 20000?
<--- Score

298. Do you designate a relationship manager for each service supplier?
<--- Score

299. What exactly do we have to achieve to become ISO 20000 compliant?
<--- Score

300. Did you relate the past experience to the new knowledge?
<--- Score

301. Have you established a traceability system and also a procedure to respond to emergency situations?
<--- Score

302. How does the service desk notify the supplier of incidents?
<--- Score

303. Are clients entitled to access EHRs?
<--- Score

Add up total points for this section:
_____ = Total points for this section

Divided by: ______ (number of statements answered) = ______ Average score for this section

Transfer your score to the ISO 20000 Index at the beginning of the Self-Assessment.

ISO 20000 and Managing Projects, Criteria for Project Managers:

1.0 Initiating Process Group: ISO 20000

1. How well did you do?

2. Are identified risks being monitored properly, are new risks arising during the ISO 20000 project or are foreseen risks occurring?

3. At which cmmi level are software processes documented, standardized, and integrated into a standard to-be practiced process for your organization?

4. Establishment of pm office?

5. What were things that you did very well and want to do the same again on the next ISO 20000 project?

6. What were things that you need to improve?

7. The process to Manage Stakeholders is part of which process group?

8. What input will you be required to provide the ISO 20000 project team?

9. What are the required resources?

10. Were decisions made in a timely manner?

11. What will be the pressing issues of tomorrow?

12. What is the NEXT thing to do?

13. Do you understand the quality and control criteria that must be achieved for successful ISO 20000 project completion?

14. Realistic - are the desired results expressed in a way that the team will be motivated and believe that the required level of involvement will be obtained?

15. Who supports, improves, and oversees standardized processes related to the ISO 20000 projects program?

16. How can you make your needs known?

17. When are the deliverables to be generated in each phase?

18. Although the ISO 20000 project manager does not directly manage procurement and contracting activities, who does manage procurement and contracting activities in your organization then if not the PM?

19. What areas does the group agree are the biggest success on the ISO 20000 project?

20. At which stage, in a typical ISO 20000 project do stake holders have maximum influence?

1.1 Project Charter: ISO 20000

21. Why executive support?

22. When?

23. Why is a ISO 20000 project Charter used?

24. Pop quiz – which are the same inputs as in the ISO 20000 project charter?

25. Fit with other Products Compliments – Cannibalizes?

26. Why use a ISO 20000 project charter?

27. Is it an improvement over existing products?

28. What metrics could you look at?

29. What are the assigned resources?

30. Why have you chosen the aim you have set forth?

31. ISO 20000 project deliverables: what is the ISO 20000 project going to produce?

32. How do you manage integration?

33. Where and how does the team fit within your organization structure?

34. If finished, on what date did it finish?

35. How high should you set your goals?

36. What outcome, in measureable terms, are you hoping to accomplish?

37. What material?

38. Strategic fit: what is the strategic initiative identifier for this ISO 20000 project?

39. Who is the sponsor?

1.2 Stakeholder Register: ISO 20000

40. What opportunities exist to provide communications?

41. How big is the gap?

42. What are the major ISO 20000 project milestones requiring communications or providing communications opportunities?

43. What is the power of the stakeholder?

44. How much influence do they have on the ISO 20000 project?

45. How should employers make voices heard?

46. What & Why?

47. How will reports be created?

48. Who are the stakeholders?

49. Is your organization ready for change?

50. Who wants to talk about Security?

51. Who is managing stakeholder engagement?

1.3 Stakeholder Analysis Matrix: ISO 20000

52. How will the stakeholder directly benefit from the ISO 20000 project and how will this affect the stakeholders motivation?

53. What is social & public accountability ?

54. Who has control over whom?

55. How much do resources cost?

56. It developments?

57. Partnerships, agencies, distribution?

58. Who is most dependent on the resources at stake?

59. Business and product development?

60. Are the required specifications for products or services changing?

61. Financial reserves, likely returns?

62. Partnership opportunities/synergies?

63. What are the mechanisms of public and social accountability, and how can they be made better?

64. Economy - home, abroad?

65. Loss of key staff?

66. Advantages of proposition?

67. How are you predicting what future (work)loads will be?

68. Processes, systems, it, communications?

69. Continuity, supply chain robustness?

70. Who can contribute financial or technical resources towards the work?

71. What is the stakeholders power and status in relation to the ISO 20000 project?

2.0 Planning Process Group: ISO 20000

72. In what way has the ISO 20000 project come up with innovative measures for problem-solving?

73. On which process should team members spend the most time?

74. How will you do it?

75. How well defined and documented are the ISO 20000 project management processes you chose to use?

76. You did your readings, yes?

77. How many days can task X be late in starting without affecting the ISO 20000 project completion date?

78. Have more efficient (sensitive) and appropriate measures been adopted to respond to the political and socio-cultural problems identified?

79. How well will the chosen processes produce the expected results?

80. What will you do?

81. Who are the ISO 20000 project stakeholders?

82. What factors are contributing to progress or delay

in the achievement of products and results?

83. Are work methodologies, financial instruments, etc. shared among departments, organizations and ISO 20000 projects?

84. If you are late, will anybody notice?

85. Have operating capacities been created and/or reinforced in partners?

86. How well did the chosen processes fit the needs of the ISO 20000 project?

87. What do you need to do?

88. Is the ISO 20000 project making progress in helping to achieve the set results?

89. To what extent are the participating departments coordinating with each other?

90. What is the difference between the early schedule and late schedule?

91. Do the partners have sufficient financial capacity to keep up the benefits produced by the programme?

2.1 Project Management Plan: ISO 20000

92. Is there an incremental analysis/cost effectiveness analysis of proposed mitigation features based on an approved method and using an accepted model?

93. How can you best help your organization to develop consistent practices in ISO 20000 project management planning stages?

94. Why do you manage integration?

95. Is there anything you would now do differently on your ISO 20000 project based on past experience?

96. What goes into your ISO 20000 project Charter?

97. What data/reports/tools/etc. do your PMs need?

98. When is the ISO 20000 project management plan created?

99. Is the appropriate plan selected based on your organizations objectives and evaluation criteria expressed in Principles and Guidelines policies?

100. How do you organize the costs in the ISO 20000 project management plan?

101. What are the assumptions?

102. What went wrong?

103. Was the peer (technical) review of the cost estimates duly coordinated with the cost estimate center of expertise and addressed in the review documentation and certification?

104. Do there need to be organizational changes?

105. Are the proposed ISO 20000 project purposes different than a previously authorized ISO 20000 project?

106. Will you add a schedule and diagram?

107. Did the planning effort collaborate to develop solutions that integrate expertise, policies, programs, and ISO 20000 projects across entities?

108. Does the implementation plan have an appropriate division of responsibilities?

109. Are calculations and results of analyzes essentially correct?

110. What is the business need?

2.2 Scope Management Plan: ISO 20000

111. Are the appropriate IT resources adequate to meet planned commitments?

112. Is mitigation authorized or recommended?

113. Has your organization done similar tasks before?

114. Are the ISO 20000 project plans updated on a frequent basis?

115. Do you keep stake holders informed?

116. Are alternatives safe, functional, constructible, economical, reasonable and sustainable?

117. Are changes in deliverable commitments agreed to by all affected groups & individuals?

118. What happens if scope changes?

119. Have reserves been created to address risks?

120. Organizational unit (e.g., department, team, or person) who will accept responsibility for satisfactory completion of the item?

121. Have all necessary approvals been obtained?

122. Are the budget estimates reasonable?

123. What are the risks that could significantly affect procuring consultant staff for the ISO 20000 project?

124. Is a pmo (ISO 20000 project management office) in place and provide oversight to the ISO 20000 project?

125. Are the schedule estimates reasonable given the ISO 20000 project?

126. Does the ISO 20000 project have a Quality Culture?

127. Is there a formal set of procedures supporting Stakeholder Management?

128. Does the title convey to the reader the essence of the ISO 20000 project?

129. Has appropriate allowance been made for the effect of the learning curve on all personnel joining the ISO 20000 project who do not have the required prior industry, functional & technical expertise?

2.3 Requirements Management Plan: ISO 20000

130. Will the contractors involved take full responsibility?

131. Do you have price sheets and a methodology for determining the total proposal cost?

132. How often will the reporting occur?

133. Could inaccurate or incomplete requirements in this ISO 20000 project create a serious risk for the business?

134. Will you use an assessment of the ISO 20000 project environment as a tool to discover risk to the requirements process?

135. Do you have an appropriate arrangement for meetings?

136. Do you have an agreed upon process for alerting the ISO 20000 project Manager if a request for change in requirements leads to a product scope change?

137. How will the requirements become prioritized?

138. Which hardware or software, related to, or as outcome of the ISO 20000 project is new to your organization?

139. Who will initially review the ISO 20000 project

work or products to ensure it meets the applicable acceptance criteria?

140. Who will finally present the work or product(s) for acceptance?

141. How do you know that you have done this right?

142. How will the information be distributed?

143. After the requirements are gathered and set forth on the requirements register, theyre little more than a laundry list of items. Some may be duplicates, some might conflict with others and some will be too broad or too vague to understand. Describe how the requirements will be analyzed. Who will perform the analysis?

144. Who came up with this requirement?

145. Will you use tracing to help understand the impact of a change in requirements?

146. Who is responsible for quantifying the ISO 20000 project requirements?

147. What went right?

148. Will you have access to stakeholders when you need them?

149. Who has the authority to reject ISO 20000 project requirements?

2.4 Requirements Documentation: ISO 20000

150. Who provides requirements?

151. Basic work/business process; high-level, what is being touched?

152. How does the proposed ISO 20000 project contribute to the overall objectives of your organization?

153. How can you document system requirements?

154. Consistency. are there any requirements conflicts?

155. What are the potential disadvantages/ advantages?

156. Completeness. are all functions required by the customer included?

157. What is the risk associated with cost and schedule?

158. Do your constraints stand?

159. Verifiability. can the requirements be checked?

160. Is new technology needed?

161. Is the requirement properly understood?

162. What are the acceptance criteria?

163. How to document system requirements?

164. Where are business rules being captured?

165. What is your Elevator Speech?

166. What are current process problems?

167. What will be the integration problems?

168. How do you get the user to tell you what they want?

169. How will they be documented / shared?

2.5 Requirements Traceability Matrix: ISO 20000

170. How will it affect the stakeholders personally in career?

171. How do you manage scope?

172. What is the WBS?

173. Do you have a clear understanding of all subcontracts in place?

174. Why do you manage scope?

175. Why use a WBS?

176. Is there a requirements traceability process in place?

177. What are the chronologies, contingencies, consequences, criteria?

178. Will you use a Requirements Traceability Matrix?

179. How small is small enough?

180. What percentage of ISO 20000 projects are producing traceability matrices between requirements and other work products?

181. Describe the process for approving requirements so they can be added to the traceability matrix and

ISO 20000 project work can be performed. Will the ISO 20000 project requirements become approved in writing?

2.6 Project Scope Statement: ISO 20000

182. Have you been able to thoroughly document the ISO 20000 projects assumptions and constraints?

183. Is the ISO 20000 project sponsor function identified and defined?

184. Who will you recommend approve the change, and when do you recommend the change reviews occur?

185. Has everyone approved the ISO 20000 projects scope statement?

186. Have the reports to be produced, distributed, and filed been defined?

187. Is there a Quality Assurance Plan documented and filed?

188. Will an issue form be in use?

189. Is the scope of your ISO 20000 project well defined?

190. Is there a baseline plan against which to measure progress?

191. Risks?

192. What is the most common tool for helping define

the detail?

193. Elements of scope management that deal with concept development ?

194. Is the quality function identified and assigned?

195. Is the ISO 20000 project manager qualified and experienced in ISO 20000 project management?

196. Will all ISO 20000 project issues be unconditionally tracked through the issue resolution process?

197. Are there specific processes you will use to evaluate and approve/reject changes?

198. Do you anticipate new stakeholders joining the ISO 20000 project over time?

199. Write a brief purpose statement for this ISO 20000 project. Include a business justification statement. What is the product of this ISO 20000 project?

2.7 Assumption and Constraint Log: ISO 20000

200. Are best practices and metrics employed to identify issues, progress, performance, etc.?

201. Are there cosmetic errors that hinder readability and comprehension?

202. Are there standards for code development?

203. What is positive about the current process?

204. Do you know what your customers expectations are regarding this process?

205. Is there a Steering Committee in place?

206. Was the document/deliverable developed per the appropriate or required standards (for example, Institute of Electrical and Electronics Engineers standards)?

207. Can the requirements be traced to the appropriate components of the solution, as well as test scripts?

208. Is the amount of effort justified by the anticipated value of forming a new process?

209. After observing execution of process, is it in compliance with the documented Plan?

210. What does an audit system look like?

211. Is there documentation of system capability requirements, data requirements, environment requirements, security requirements, and computer and hardware requirements?

212. How many ISO 20000 project staff does this specific process affect?

213. Does a documented ISO 20000 project organizational policy & plan (i.e. governance model) exist?

214. Violation trace: why ?

215. Has the approach and development strategy of the ISO 20000 project been defined, documented and accepted by the appropriate stakeholders?

216. What if failure during recovery?

217. Were the system requirements formally reviewed prior to initiating the design phase?

218. Have all stakeholders been identified?

219. What to do at recovery?

2.8 Work Breakdown Structure: ISO 20000

220. Do you need another level?

221. What has to be done?

222. Is the work breakdown structure (wbs) defined and is the scope of the ISO 20000 project clear with assigned deliverable owners?

223. How much detail?

224. Is it still viable?

225. Why would you develop a Work Breakdown Structure?

226. When would you develop a Work Breakdown Structure?

227. When does it have to be done?

228. Where does it take place?

229. Can you make it?

230. When do you stop?

231. What is the probability that the ISO 20000 project duration will exceed xx weeks?

232. Who has to do it?

233. How big is a work-package?

234. What is the probability of completing the ISO 20000 project in less that xx days?

235. How many levels?

2.9 WBS Dictionary: ISO 20000

236. Are records maintained to show how undistributed budgets are controlled?

237. Are current budgets resulting from changes to the authorized work and/or internal replanning, reconcilable to original budgets for specified reporting items?

238. Are records maintained to show full accountability for all material purchased for the contract, including the residual inventory?

239. Should you have a test for each code module?

240. Are procedures in existence that control replanning of unopened work packages, and are corresponding procedures adhered to?

241. Are the bases and rates for allocating costs from each indirect pool to commercial work consistent with the already stated used to allocate corresponding costs to Government contracts?

242. Is cost performance measurement at the point in time most suitable for the category of material involved, and no earlier than the time of actual receipt of material?

243. Are the wbs and organizational levels for application of the ISO 20000 projected overhead costs identified?

244. Are meaningful indicators identified for use in measuring the status of cost and schedule performance?

245. Changes in the overhead pool and/or organization structures?

246. What are you counting on?

247. Does the contractors system provide unit costs, equivalent unit or lot costs in terms of labor, material, other direct, and indirect costs?

248. Does the contractor have procedures which permit identification of recurring or non-recurring costs as necessary?

249. Major functional areas of contract effort?

250. Are current work performance indicators and goals relatable to original goals as modified by contractual changes, replanning, and reprogramming actions?

251. Software specification, development, integration, and testing, licenses ?

252. Contemplated overhead expenditure for each period based on the best information currently available?

253. Can the contractor substantiate work package and planning package budgets?

254. The ISO 20000 projected business base for each period?

2.10 Schedule Management Plan: ISO 20000

255. What strengths do you have?

256. Are written status reports provided on a designated frequent basis?

257. Have adequate resources been provided by management to ensure ISO 20000 project success?

258. Has a quality assurance plan been developed for the ISO 20000 project?

259. Are there any activities or deliverables being added or gold-plated that could be dropped or scaled back without falling short of the original requirement?

260. Are cause and effect determined for risks when they occur?

261. Are vendor contract reports, reviews and visits conducted periodically?

262. List all schedule constraints here. Must the ISO 20000 project be complete by a specified date?

263. Are ISO 20000 project team members committed fulltime?

264. Are the constraints or deadlines associated with the task accurate?

265. Does the schedule have reasonable float?

266. Why time management?

267. Has a ISO 20000 project Communications Plan been developed?

268. Is quality monitored from the perspective of the customers needs and expectations?

269. Is there an onboarding process in place?

270. Is the ims used by all levels of management for ISO 20000 project implementation and control?

271. Are the ISO 20000 project plans updated on a frequent basis?

272. Were stakeholders aware and supportive of the principles and practices of modern software estimation?

273. Are tasks tracked by hours?

2.11 Activity List: ISO 20000

274. What is the probability the ISO 20000 project can be completed in xx weeks?

275. What did not go as well?

276. How detailed should a ISO 20000 project get?

277. How should ongoing costs be monitored to try to keep the ISO 20000 project within budget?

278. In what sequence?

279. Who will perform the work?

280. How will it be performed?

281. For other activities, how much delay can be tolerated?

282. How difficult will it be to do specific activities on this ISO 20000 project?

283. What went well?

284. The wbs is developed as part of a joint planning session. and how do you know that youhave done this right?

285. What will be performed?

286. Can you determine the activity that must finish, before this activity can start?

287. Where will it be performed?

288. What is your organizations history in doing similar activities?

289. Is infrastructure setup part of your ISO 20000 project?

290. How much slack is available in the ISO 20000 project?

2.12 Activity Attributes: ISO 20000

291. Were there other ways you could have organized the data to achieve similar results?

292. Time for overtime?

293. Resources to accomplish the work?

294. Is there a trend during the year?

295. Resource is assigned to?

296. How many resources do you need to complete the work scope within a limit of X number of days?

297. How many days do you need to complete the work scope with a limit of X number of resources?

298. Where else does it apply?

299. What is missing?

300. Are the required resources available or need to be acquired?

301. Can you re-assign any activities to another resource to resolve an over-allocation?

302. How difficult will it be to do specific activities on this ISO 20000 project?

303. Have constraints been applied to the start and finish milestones for the phases?

304. What activity do you think you should spend the most time on?

305. How else could the items be grouped?

306. Do you feel very comfortable with your prediction?

307. Which method produces the more accurate cost assignment?

2.13 Milestone List: ISO 20000

308. How soon can the activity start?

309. Can you derive how soon can the whole ISO 20000 project finish?

310. Level of the Innovation?

311. Milestone pages should display the UserID of the person who added the milestone. Does a report or query exist that provides this audit information?

312. How will you get the word out to customers?

313. When will the ISO 20000 project be complete?

314. Do you foresee any technical risks or developmental challenges?

315. Describe your organizations strengths and core competencies. What factors will make your organization succeed?

316. Insurmountable weaknesses?

317. How will the milestone be verified?

318. Identify critical paths (one or more) and which activities are on the critical path?

319. How late can each activity be finished and started?

320. How soon can the activity finish?

321. How do you manage time?

322. Vital contracts and partners?

323. What are your competitors vulnerabilities?

324. Legislative effects?

2.14 Network Diagram: ISO 20000

325. Can you calculate the confidence level?

326. What job or jobs precede it?

327. Are the required resources available?

328. Will crashing x weeks return more in benefits than it costs?

329. What job or jobs could run concurrently?

330. If a current contract exists, can you provide the vendor name, contract start, and contract expiration date?

331. Are you on time?

332. Which type of network diagram allows you to depict four types of dependencies?

333. Where do schedules come from?

334. What is the completion time?

335. What can be done concurrently?

336. What is the probability of completing the ISO 20000 project in less that xx days?

337. What controls the start and finish of a job?

338. Review the logical flow of the network diagram.

Take a look at which activities you have first and then sequence the activities. Do they make sense?

339. Exercise: what is the probability that the ISO 20000 project duration will exceed xx weeks?

340. What activity must be completed immediately before this activity can start?

341. Where do you schedule uncertainty time?

342. If the ISO 20000 project network diagram cannot change and you have extra personnel resources, what is the BEST thing to do?

343. What to do and When?

2.15 Activity Resource Requirements: ISO 20000

344. Do you use tools like decomposition and rolling-wave planning to produce the activity list and other outputs?

345. What are constraints that you might find during the Human Resource Planning process?

346. What is the Work Plan Standard?

347. How do you handle petty cash?

348. Why do you do that?

349. How many signatures do you require on a check and does this match what is in your policy and procedures?

350. Are there unresolved issues that need to be addressed?

351. Other support in specific areas?

352. Which logical relationship does the PDM use most often?

353. Anything else?

354. When does monitoring begin?

355. Organizational Applicability?

356. Is there anything planned that does not need to be here?

2.16 Resource Breakdown Structure: ISO 20000

357. Changes based on input from stakeholders?

358. What can you do to improve productivity?

359. What is the primary purpose of the human resource plan?

360. Who needs what information?

361. Why do you do it?

362. When do they need the information?

363. Who delivers the information?

364. The list could probably go on, but, the thing that you would most like to know is, How long & How much?

365. What is the number one predictor of a groups productivity?

366. Which resources should be in the resource pool?

367. Who will use the system?

368. Which resource planning tool provides information on resource responsibility and accountability?

369. Any changes from stakeholders?

370. What are the requirements for resource data?

371. What is the difference between % Complete and % work?

372. What is ISO 20000 project communication management?

373. Goals for the ISO 20000 project. What is each stakeholders desired outcome for the ISO 20000 project?

2.17 Activity Duration Estimates: ISO 20000

374. What type of contract was used and why?

375. Which best describes how this affects the ISO 20000 project?

376. What is the BEST thing for the ISO 20000 project manager to do?

377. What do you think about the WBSs for them?

378. How does poking fun at technical professionals communications skills impact the industry and educational programs?

379. How many different communications channels does a ISO 20000 project team with six people have?

380. What type of activity sequencing method is required for corresponding activities?

381. How have experts such as Deming, Juran, Crosby, and Taguchi affected the quality movement and todays use of Six Sigma?

382. How does ISO 20000 project management relate to other disciplines?

383. What is involved in the solicitation process?

384. What is the career outlook for ISO 20000 project

managers in information technology?

385. What do you think the real problem was in this case?

386. Is a ISO 20000 project charter created once a ISO 20000 project is formally recognized?

387. Are adjustments implemented to correct or prevent defects?

388. Briefly describe some key events in the history of ISO 20000 project management. What ISO 20000 project was the first to use modern ISO 20000 project management?

389. Are the causes of all variances identified?

390. Are steps identified by which ISO 20000 project documents may be changed?

391. Which is the BEST thing to do to try to complete a ISO 20000 project two days earlier?

392. What should be done NEXT?

393. Are tools and techniques defined for gathering, integrating and distributing ISO 20000 project outputs?

2.18 Duration Estimating Worksheet: ISO 20000

394. Small or large ISO 20000 project?

395. What questions do you have?

396. Science = process: remember the scientific method?

397. Why estimate time and cost?

398. Is this operation cost effective?

399. How should ongoing costs be monitored to try to keep the ISO 20000 project within budget?

400. Done before proceeding with this activity or what can be done concurrently?

401. Is the ISO 20000 project responsive to community need?

402. What is next?

403. What is the total time required to complete the ISO 20000 project if no delays occur?

404. What utility impacts are there?

405. What is cost and ISO 20000 project cost management?

406. Value pocket identification & quantification what are value pockets?

407. Will the ISO 20000 project collaborate with the local community and leverage resources?

408. When do the individual activities need to start and finish?

409. Is a construction detail attached (to aid in explanation)?

410. What info is needed?

411. Can the ISO 20000 project be constructed as planned?

2.19 Project Schedule: ISO 20000

412. Are key risk mitigation strategies added to the ISO 20000 project schedule?

413. Have all ISO 20000 project delays been adequately accounted for, communicated to all stakeholders and adjustments made in overall ISO 20000 project schedule?

414. How does a ISO 20000 project get to be a year late ?

415. Activity charts and bar charts are graphical representations of a ISO 20000 project schedule ...how do they differ?

416. How much slack is available in the ISO 20000 project?

417. How do you know that youhave done this right?

418. Your ISO 20000 project management plan results in a ISO 20000 project schedule that is too long. If the ISO 20000 project network diagram cannot change and you have extra personnel resources, what is the BEST thing to do?

419. Why is software ISO 20000 project disaster so common?

420. How closely did the initial ISO 20000 project Schedule compare with the actual schedule?

421. Why do you need schedules?

422. What does that mean?

423. How can you fix it?

424. Is ISO 20000 project work proceeding in accordance with the original ISO 20000 project schedule?

425. Is there a Schedule Management Plan that establishes the criteria and activities for developing, monitoring and controlling the ISO 20000 project schedule?

426. Is the ISO 20000 project schedule available for all ISO 20000 project team members to review?

427. What is risk?

428. How can you shorten the schedule?

429. Does the condition or event threaten the ISO 20000 projects objectives in any ways?

430. Is the structure for tracking the ISO 20000 project schedule well defined and assigned to a specific individual?

431. Did the final product meet or exceed user expectations?

2.20 Cost Management Plan: ISO 20000

432. Are software metrics formally captured, analyzed and used as a basis for other ISO 20000 project estimates?

433. Are parking lot items captured?

434. ISO 20000 project definition & scope?

435. Is your organization certified as a supplier, wholesaler, regular dealer, or manufacturer of corresponding products/supplies?

436. Cost tracking and performance analysis - How will cost tracking and performance analysis be accomplished?

437. Change types and category - What are the types of changes and what are the techniques to report and control changes?

438. Cost / benefit analysis?

439. Are change requests logged and managed?

440. Is an industry recognized mechanized support tool(s) being used for ISO 20000 project scheduling & tracking?

441. Is the schedule updated on a periodic basis?

442. Published materials?

443. Contractors scope – how will contractors scope be defined when contracts are let?

444. Has the scope management document been updated and distributed to help prevent scope creep?

445. Cost estimate preparation – What cost estimates will be prepared during the ISO 20000 project phases?

446. Is it a ISO 20000 project?

447. Have all unresolved risks been documented?

448. Is a pmo (ISO 20000 project management office) in place and provide oversight to the ISO 20000 project?

449. Is a payment system in place with proper reviews and approvals?

2.21 Activity Cost Estimates: ISO 20000

450. Would you hire them again?

451. How many activities should you have?

452. Is costing method consistent with study goals?

453. Does the estimator estimate by task or by person?

454. What communication items need improvement?

455. What makes a good activity description?

456. Can you change your activities?

457. The impact and what actions were taken?

458. What is the activity inventory?

459. Were escalated issues resolved promptly?

460. How difficult will it be to do specific tasks on the ISO 20000 project?

461. What is your organizations history in doing similar tasks?

462. How do you manage cost?

463. What is included in indirect cost being allocated?

464. What happens if you cannot produce the documentation for the single audit?

465. What is the activity recast of the budget?

466. Did the ISO 20000 project team have the right skills?

467. What makes a good expected result statement?

468. When do you enter into PPM?

469. Can you delete activities or make them inactive?

2.22 Cost Estimating Worksheet: ISO 20000

470. Identify the timeframe necessary to monitor progress and collect data to determine how the selected measure has changed?

471. Does the ISO 20000 project provide innovative ways for stakeholders to overcome obstacles or deliver better outcomes?

472. Ask: are others positioned to know, are others credible, and will others cooperate?

473. Can a trend be established from historical performance data on the selected measure and are the criteria for using trend analysis or forecasting methods met?

474. What can be included?

475. Is it feasible to establish a control group arrangement?

476. What will others want?

477. What happens to any remaining funds not used?

478. Who is best positioned to know and assist in identifying corresponding factors?

479. What is the estimated labor cost today based upon this information?

480. How will the results be shared and to whom?

481. Is the ISO 20000 project responsive to community need?

482. Will the ISO 20000 project collaborate with the local community and leverage resources?

483. What additional ISO 20000 project(s) could be initiated as a result of this ISO 20000 project?

484. What costs are to be estimated?

485. What is the purpose of estimating?

2.23 Cost Baseline: ISO 20000

486. Has operations management formally accepted responsibility for operating and maintaining the product(s) or service(s) delivered by the ISO 20000 project?

487. On time?

488. At which frequency ?

489. Who will use corresponding metrics ?

490. What is it ?

491. If you sold 10x widgets on a day, what would the affect on profits be?

492. Verify business objectives. Are others appropriate, and well-articulated?

493. Eac -estimate at completion, what is the total job expected to cost?

494. Vac -variance at completion, how much over/ under budget do you expect to be?

495. Impact to environment?

496. Is there anything you need from upper management in order to be successful?

497. What do you want to measure ?

498. Have all approved changes to the ISO 20000 project requirement been identified and impact on the performance, cost, and schedule baselines documented?

499. Have the resources used by the ISO 20000 project been reassigned to other units or ISO 20000 projects?

500. Does the suggested change request seem to represent a necessary enhancement to the product?

501. How will cost estimates be used?

502. Is request in line with priorities?

503. Has the documentation relating to operation and maintenance of the product(s) or service(s) been delivered to, and accepted by, operations management?

2.24 Quality Management Plan: ISO 20000

504. How are data handled when a test is not run per specification?

505. Who is responsible?

506. What is quality planning ?

507. If it is out of compliance, should the process be amended or should the Plan be amended?

508. Results Available?

509. How relevant is this attribute to this ISO 20000 project or audit?

510. How do you decide what information to record?

511. When reporting to different audiences, do you vary the form or type of report?

512. What are your organizations current levels and trends for the already stated measures related to customer satisfaction/ dissatisfaction and product/ service performance?

513. Do you periodically review your data quality system to see that it is up to date and appropriate?

514. How do you decide who is responsible for signing the data reports?

515. Who do you send data to?

516. Have adequate resources been provided by management to ensure ISO 20000 project success?

517. How do senior leaders create your organizational focus on customers and other stakeholders?

518. What has the QM Collaboration done?

519. Methodology followed?

520. Are there trends or hot spots?

521. Modifications to the requirements?

522. Are there ways to reduce the time it takes to get something approved?

2.25 Quality Metrics: ISO 20000

523. What does this tell us?

524. Where is quality now?

525. How effective are your security tests?

526. Do you know how much profit a 10% decrease in waste would generate?

527. What level of statistical confidence do you use?

528. Did evaluation start on time?

529. Should a modifier be included?

530. Was the overall quality better or worse than previous products?

531. What method of measurement do you use?

532. What if the biggest risk to your business were the already stated people who do not complain?

533. Which are the right metrics to use?

534. What metrics are important and most beneficial to measure?

535. Has it met internal or external standards?

536. Was material distributed on time?

537. Product Availability ?

538. Is there alignment within your organization on definitions?

539. Have alternatives been defined in the event that failure occurs?

540. Has trace of defects been initiated?

541. Filter visualizations of interest?

2.26 Process Improvement Plan: ISO 20000

542. What personnel are the change agents for your initiative?

543. If a process improvement framework is being used, which elements will help the problems and goals listed?

544. Have storage and access mechanisms and procedures been determined?

545. Are there forms and procedures to collect and record the data?

546. Where do you want to be?

547. What is quality and how will you ensure it?

548. Where do you focus?

549. What is the test-cycle concept?

550. Are you meeting the quality standards?

551. What actions are needed to address the problems and achieve the goals?

552. Does your process ensure quality?

553. What lessons have you learned so far?

554. What personnel are the champions for the initiative?

555. Everyone agrees on what process improvement is, right?

556. Modeling current processes is great, and will you ever see a return on that investment?

557. What is the return on investment?

558. Management commitment at all levels?

559. Are you making progress on the goals?

560. Are you making progress on the improvement framework?

2.27 Responsibility Assignment Matrix: ISO 20000

561. Do all the identified groups or people really need to be consulted?

562. Are the requirements for all items of overhead established by rational, traceable processes?

563. Does a missing responsibility indicate that the current ISO 20000 project is not yet fully understood?

564. Most people let you know when others re too busy, and are others really too busy?

565. Is the entire contract planned in time-phased control accounts to the extent practicable?

566. Do work packages consist of discrete tasks which are adequately described?

567. What are the constraints?

568. Too many as: does a proper segregation of duties exist?

569. Are people afraid to let you know when others are under allocated?

570. No rs: if a task has no one listed as responsible, who is getting the job done?

571. How can this help you with team building?

572. Are overhead cost budgets established for each organization which has authority to incur overhead costs?

573. Identify and isolate causes of favorable and unfavorable cost and schedule variances?

574. If a role has only Signing-off, or only Communicating responsibility and has no Performing, Accountable, or Monitoring responsibility, is it necessary?

575. Does the contractors system provide unit or lot costs when applicable?

576. Budgeted cost for work scheduled?

577. Are significant decision points, constraints, and interfaces identified as key milestones?

578. Which ISO 20000 project management knowledge area is least mature?

2.28 Roles and Responsibilities: ISO 20000

579. What should you do now to prepare for your career 5+ years from now?

580. What are your major roles and responsibilities in the area of performance measurement and assessment?

581. Who is responsible for implementation activities and where will the functions, roles and responsibilities be defined?

582. What specific behaviors did you observe?

583. Where are you most strong as a supervisor?

584. What should you do now to prepare yourself for a promotion, increased responsibilities or a different job?

585. Does the team have access to and ability to use data analysis tools?

586. Who is responsible for each task?

587. What expectations were met?

588. Are ISO 20000 project team roles and responsibilities identified and documented?

589. Be specific; avoid generalities. Thank you and

great work alone are insufficient. What exactly do you appreciate and why?

590. Are your policies supportive of a culture of quality data?

591. Does your vision/mission support a culture of quality data?

592. Implementation of actions: Who are the responsible units?

593. Is the data complete?

594. How well did the ISO 20000 project Team understand the expectations of specific roles and responsibilities?

595. To decide whether to use a quality measurement, ask how will you know when it is achieved?

596. What is working well?

597. What areas of supervision are challenging for you?

598. What should you highlight for improvement?

2.29 Human Resource Management Plan: ISO 20000

599. Are there checklists created to determine if all quality processes are followed?

600. Are all resource assumptions documented?

601. Is the steering committee active in ISO 20000 project oversight?

602. Is the manpower level sufficient to meet the future business requirements?

603. Has the budget been baselined?

604. Have the key functions and capabilities been defined and assigned to each release or iteration?

605. Timeline and milestones?

606. Has a sponsor been identified?

607. Are people motivated to meet the current and future challenges?

608. Has a resource management plan been created?

609. How complete is the human resource management plan?

610. Is it standard practice to formally commit stakeholders to the ISO 20000 project via

agreements?

611. Quality assurance overheads?

612. Based on your ISO 20000 project communication management plan, what worked well?

613. Are schedule deliverables actually delivered?

2.30 Communications Management Plan: ISO 20000

614. Why do you manage communications?

615. Do you then often overlook a key stakeholder or stakeholder group?

616. Are you constantly rushing from meeting to meeting?

617. What communications method?

618. What is the stakeholders level of authority?

619. Why is stakeholder engagement important?

620. Are the stakeholders getting the information others need, are others consulted, are concerns addressed?

621. Are there potential barriers between the team and the stakeholder?

622. What is ISO 20000 project communications management?

623. What does the stakeholder need from the team?

624. In your work, how much time is spent on stakeholder identification?

625. What are the interrelationships?

626. Which stakeholders are thought leaders, influences, or early adopters?

627. Which team member will work with each stakeholder?

628. Will messages be directly related to the release strategy or phases of the ISO 20000 project?

629. What to learn?

630. Who did you turn to if you had questions?

631. Can you think of other people who might have concerns or interests?

632. How often do you engage with stakeholders?

633. Where do team members get information?

2.31 Risk Management Plan: ISO 20000

634. How will the ISO 20000 project know if your organizations risk response actions were effective?

635. Is the customer willing to participate in reviews?

636. If you can not fix it, how do you do it differently?

637. Are the participants able to keep up with the workload?

638. Technology risk: is the ISO 20000 project technically feasible?

639. Is there additional information that would make you more confident about your analysis?

640. Are end-users enthusiastically committed to the ISO 20000 project and the system/product to be built?

641. Maximize short-term return on investment?

642. What can you do to minimize the impact if it does?

643. What other risks are created by choosing an avoidance strategy?

644. Management -what contingency plans do you have if the risk becomes a reality?

645. Risk documentation: what reporting formats and processes will be used for risk management activities?

646. Is a software ISO 20000 project management tool available?

647. Was an original risk assessment/risk management plan completed?

648. Market risk -will the new service or product be useful to your organization or marketable to others?

649. Are team members trained in the use of the tools?

650. What would you do differently?

651. Risks should be identified during which phase of ISO 20000 project management life cycle?

652. My ISO 20000 project leader has suddenly left your organization, what do you do?

653. Internal technical and management reviews?

2.32 Risk Register: ISO 20000

654. Having taken action, how did the responses effect change, and where is the ISO 20000 project now?

655. How could corresponding Risk affect the ISO 20000 project in terms of cost and schedule?

656. What are the main aims, objectives of the policy, strategy, or service and the intended outcomes?

657. Schedule impact/severity estimated range (workdays) assume the event happens, what is the potential impact?

658. What are your key risks/show istoppers and what is being done to manage them?

659. What evidence do you have to justify the likelihood score of the risk (audit, incident report, claim, complaints, inspection, internal review)?

660. What would the impact to the ISO 20000 project objectives be should the risk arise?

661. Do you require further engagement?

662. What should the audit role be in establishing a risk management process?

663. User involvement: do you have the right users?

664. When will it happen?

665. How is a Community Risk Register created?

666. Severity Prediction?

667. Cost/benefit – how much will the proposed mitigations cost and how does this cost compare with the potential cost of the risk event/situation should it occur?

668. Who needs to know about this?

669. What may happen or not go according to plan?

670. What are the major risks facing the ISO 20000 project?

671. When would you develop a risk register?

672. What is the appropriate level of risk management for this ISO 20000 project?

673. Are corrective measures implemented as planned?

2.33 Probability and Impact Assessment: ISO 20000

674. How are you working with risks?

675. What risks are necessary to achieve success?

676. What are the current demands of the customer?

677. What are the uncertainties associated with the technology selected for the ISO 20000 project?

678. Why has this particular mode of contracting been chosen?

679. Are there any ISO 20000 projects similar to this one in existence?

680. Does the customer understand the software process?

681. Do you have specific methods that you use for each phase of the process?

682. What will be cost of redeployment of personnel?

683. Do benefits and chances of success outweigh potential damage if success is not attained?

684. Which of your ISO 20000 projects should be selected when compared with other ISO 20000 projects?

685. How do risks change during the ISO 20000 projects life cycle?

686. What action do you usually take against risks?

687. Assumptions analysis -what assumptions have you made or been given about your ISO 20000 project?

688. When and how will the recent breakthroughs in basic research lead to commercial products?

689. Will new information become available during the ISO 20000 project?

690. What are your data sources?

691. Are tool mentors available?

692. Are testing tools available and suitable?

693. How solid is the ISO 20000 projection of competitive reaction?

2.34 Probability and Impact Matrix: ISO 20000

694. Do the people have the right combinations of skills?

695. During which risk management process is a determination to transfer a risk made?

696. Are people attending meetings and doing work?

697. How is the risk management process used in practice?

698. What are the methods to deal with risks?

699. Are enough people available?

700. What things are likely to change?

701. Do the requirements require the creation of new algorithms?

702. Can it be changed quickly?

703. Is the ISO 20000 project cutting across the entire organization?

704. Are the best people available?

705. Do requirements demand the use of new analysis, design, or testing methods?

706. What are the chances the event will occur?

707. What should be done with risks on the watch list?

708. Are the risk data complete?

709. Sensitivity analysis -which risks will have the most impact on the ISO 20000 project?

710. Premium on reliability of product?

711. Which role do you have in the ISO 20000 project?

712. What did not work so well?

2.35 Risk Data Sheet: ISO 20000

713. What actions can be taken to eliminate or remove risk?

714. During work activities could hazards exist?

715. Has a sensitivity analysis been carried out?

716. What will be the consequences if it happens?

717. What can happen?

718. What can you do?

719. Is the data sufficiently specified in terms of the type of failure being analyzed, and its frequency or probability?

720. What are your core values?

721. How reliable is the data source?

722. What are the main opportunities available to you that you should grab while you can?

723. What are the main threats to your existence?

724. If it happens, what are the consequences?

725. What do you know?

726. How can it happen?

727. What are you here for (Mission)?

728. What is the environment within which you operate (social trends, economic, community values, broad based participation, national directions etc.)?

729. What do people affected think about the need for, and practicality of preventive measures?

730. What is the chance that it will happen?

731. Whom do you serve (customers)?

2.36 Procurement Management Plan: ISO 20000

732. Have the key elements of a coherent ISO 20000 project management strategy been established?

733. Does the resource management plan include a personnel development plan?

734. Are the ISO 20000 project team members located locally to the users/stakeholders?

735. Are action items captured and managed?

736. Is the ISO 20000 project sponsor clearly communicating the business case or rationale for why this ISO 20000 project is needed?

737. Is there a set of procedures to capture, analyze and act on quality metrics?

738. Are changes in scope (deliverable commitments) agreed to by all affected groups & individuals?

739. Does the ISO 20000 project team have the right skills?

740. Has the ISO 20000 project manager been identified?

741. What are things that you need to improve?

742. Does a documented ISO 20000 project

organizational policy & plan (i.e. governance model) exist?

743. Measurable - are the targets measurable?

744. Is there a formal set of procedures supporting Issues Management?

745. Has a structured approach been used to break work effort into manageable components (WBS)?

746. ISO 20000 project Objectives?

747. Are any non-compliance issues that exist communicated to your organization?

2.37 Source Selection Criteria: ISO 20000

748. How should comments received in response to a RFP be handled?

749. When must you conduct a debriefing?

750. What should communications be used to accomplish?

751. Is there collaboration among your evaluators?

752. How long will it take for the purchase cost to be the same as the lease cost?

753. What are the guidelines regarding award without considerations?

754. What should be the contracting officers strategy?

755. What instructions should be provided regarding oral presentations?

756. When is it appropriate to conduct a preproposal conference?

757. Do you want to wait until all offerors have been evaluated?

758. Can you reasonably estimate total organization requirements for the coming year?

759. Who must be notified?

760. In order of importance, which evaluation criteria are the most critical to the determination of your overall rating?

761. How should the oral presentations be handled?

762. In which phase of the acquisition process cycle does source qualifications reside?

763. How much weight should be placed on past performance information?

764. How and when do you enter into ISO 20000 project Procurement Management?

765. How do you consolidate reviews and analysis of evaluators?

766. What are the most critical evaluation criteria that prove to be tiebreakers in the evaluation of proposals?

767. Do you have designated specific forms or worksheets?

2.38 Stakeholder Management Plan: ISO 20000

768. What action will be taken once reports have been received?

769. Are decisions captured in a decisions log?

770. Has a capability assessment been conducted?

771. Are the ISO 20000 project plans updated on a frequent basis?

772. Have ISO 20000 project team accountabilities & responsibilities been clearly defined?

773. Is ISO 20000 project status reviewed with the steering and executive teams at appropriate intervals?

774. Have process improvement efforts been completed before requirements efforts begin?

775. Have adequate resources been provided by management to ensure ISO 20000 project success?

776. Is stakeholder involvement adequate?

777. Are there procedures in place to effectively manage interdependencies with other ISO 20000 projects / systems?

778. Is a stakeholder management plan in place?

779. Is an industry recognized mechanized support tool(s) being used for ISO 20000 project scheduling & tracking?

780. Are there checklists created to demine if all quality processes are followed?

781. Are formal code reviews conducted?

782. Is it standard practice to formally commit stakeholders to the ISO 20000 project via agreements?

783. Are ISO 20000 project team members involved in detailed estimating and scheduling?

784. Was the scope definition used in task sequencing?

785. Are communication systems currently in place appropriate?

786. Has the ISO 20000 project scope been baselined?

2.39 Change Management Plan: ISO 20000

787. What prerequisite knowledge do corresponding groups need?

788. Has the training co-ordinator been provided with the training details and put in place the necessary arrangements?

789. Has a training need analysis been carried out?

790. What is going to be done differently?

791. Would you need to tailor a special message for each segment of the audience?

792. Has the relevant business unit been notified of installation and support requirements?

793. What does a resilient organization look like?

794. Different application of an existing process?

795. Are there any restrictions on who can receive the communications?

796. Will a different work structure focus people on what is important?

797. How do you know the requirements you documented are the right ones?

798. Why is it important?

799. How much ISO 20000 project management is needed?

800. What do you expect the target audience to do, say, think or feel as a result of this communication?

801. Will all field readiness criteria have been practically met prior to training roll-out?

802. What are the training strategies?

803. What new behaviours are required?

804. What risks may occur upfront?

805. Is there support for this application(s) and are the details available for distribution?

806. What policies and procedures need to be changed?

3.0 Executing Process Group: ISO 20000

807. How well did the chosen processes fit the needs of the ISO 20000 project?

808. Specific - is the objective clear in terms of what, how, when, and where the situation will be changed?

809. What good practices or successful experiences or transferable examples have been identified?

810. Do the products created live up to the necessary quality?

811. Mitigate. what will you do to minimize the impact should a risk event occur?

812. What is the difference between using brainstorming and the Delphi technique for risk identification?

813. What is the critical path for this ISO 20000 project and how long is it?

814. How do you control progress of your ISO 20000 project?

815. What type of information goes in the quality assurance plan?

816. How could stakeholders negatively impact your ISO 20000 project?

817. In what way has the program come up with innovative measures for problem-solving?

818. Who will be the main sponsor?

819. What areas does the group agree are the biggest success on the ISO 20000 project?

820. What are deliverables of your ISO 20000 project?

821. How will professionals learn what is expected from them what the deliverables are?

822. How well did the chosen processes produce the expected results?

823. Is the ISO 20000 project performing better or worse than planned?

824. Based on your ISO 20000 project communication management plan, what worked well?

825. What is in place for ensuring adequate change control on ISO 20000 projects that involve outside contracts?

3.1 Team Member Status Report: ISO 20000

826. Does every department have to have a ISO 20000 project Manager on staff?

827. Are the attitudes of staff regarding ISO 20000 project work improving?

828. Why is it to be done?

829. How much risk is involved?

830. How can you make it practical?

831. Does your organization have the means (staff, money, contract, etc.) to produce or to acquire the product, good, or service?

832. Are the products of your organizations ISO 20000 projects meeting customers objectives?

833. How does this product, good, or service meet the needs of the ISO 20000 project and your organization as a whole?

834. Do you have an Enterprise ISO 20000 project Management Office (EPMO)?

835. How it is to be done?

836. Are your organizations ISO 20000 projects more successful over time?

837. Does the product, good, or service already exist within your organization?

838. The problem with Reward & Recognition Programs is that the truly deserving people all too often get left out. How can you make it practical?

839. When a teams productivity and success depend on collaboration and the efficient flow of information, what generally fails them?

840. How will resource planning be done?

841. Will the staff do training or is that done by a third party?

842. Is there evidence that staff is taking a more professional approach toward management of your organizations ISO 20000 projects?

843. What specific interest groups do you have in place?

844. What is to be done?

3.2 Change Request: ISO 20000

845. What are the basic mechanics of the Change Advisory Board (CAB)?

846. Are you implementing itil processes?

847. Should a more thorough impact analysis be conducted?

848. Who is included in the change control team?

849. How to get changes (code) out in a timely manner?

850. Does the schedule include ISO 20000 project management time and change request analysis time?

851. How does your organization control changes before and after software is released to a customer?

852. How does a team identify the discrete elements of a configuration?

853. Who needs to approve change requests?

854. Why do you want to have a change control system?

855. How are the measures for carrying out the change established?

856. What are the Impacts to your organization?

857. Who is responsible to authorize changes?

858. Have all related configuration items been properly updated?

859. Will this change conflict with other requirements changes (e.g., lead to conflicting operational scenarios)?

860. How can you ensure that changes have been made properly?

861. Screen shots or attachments included in a Change Request?

862. Change request coordination ?

863. What mechanism is used to appraise others of changes that are made?

3.3 Change Log: ISO 20000

864. Will the ISO 20000 project fail if the change request is not executed?

865. Is the change backward compatible without limitations?

866. Is the requested change request a result of changes in other ISO 20000 project(s)?

867. Who initiated the change request?

868. Does the suggested change request represent a desired enhancement to the products functionality?

869. Where do changes come from?

870. When was the request approved?

871. Is the change request open, closed or pending?

872. Is this a mandatory replacement?

873. How does this change affect the timeline of the schedule?

874. Do the described changes impact on the integrity or security of the system?

875. How does this relate to the standards developed for specific business processes?

876. Is the submitted change a new change or a

modification of a previously approved change?

877. How does this change affect scope?

878. When was the request submitted?

879. Is the change request within ISO 20000 project scope?

3.4 Decision Log: ISO 20000

880. Decision-making process; how will the team make decisions?

881. How effective is maintaining the log at facilitating organizational learning?

882. At what point in time does loss become unacceptable?

883. What are the cost implications?

884. Does anything need to be adjusted?

885. What makes you different or better than others companies selling the same thing?

886. Do strategies and tactics aimed at less than full control reduce the costs of management or simply shift the cost burden?

887. With whom was the decision shared or considered?

888. How do you know when you are achieving it?

889. How does provision of information, both in terms of content and presentation, influence acceptance of alternative strategies?

890. It becomes critical to track and periodically revisit both operational effectiveness; Are you noticing all that you need to, and are you interpreting what you

see effectively?

891. What is your overall strategy for quality control / quality assurance procedures?

892. How does the use a Decision Support System influence the strategies/tactics or costs?

893. How consolidated and comprehensive a story can you tell by capturing currently available incident data in a central location and through a log of key decisions during an incident?

894. What was the rationale for the decision?

895. Which variables make a critical difference?

896. What is the average size of your matters in an applicable measurement?

897. Who will be given a copy of this document and where will it be kept?

898. Who is the decisionmaker?

899. Linked to original objective?

3.5 Quality Audit: ISO 20000

900. Are all employees including salespersons made aware that they must report all complaints received from any source for inclusion in the complaint handling system?

901. How does your organization know that the quality of its supervisors is appropriately effective and constructive?

902. How does your organization know that its staff embody the core knowledge, skills and characteristics for which it wishes to be recognized?

903. How does your organization know that its staffing profile is optimally aligned with the capability requirements implicit (or explicit) in its Strategic Plan?

904. For each device to be reconditioned, are device specifications, such as appropriate engineering drawings, component specifications and software specifications, maintained?

905. How does your organization know that its relationships with the community at large are appropriately effective and constructive?

906. How does your organization know that the support for its staff is appropriately effective and constructive?

907. How does your organization know that its Strategic Plan is providing the best guidance for the

future of your organization?

908. What happens if your organization fails its Quality Audit?

909. How does your organization know that its relationships with other relevant organizations are appropriately effective and constructive?

910. What data about organizational performance is routinely collected and reported?

911. Why are you trying to do it?

912. How does your organization know that its system for examining work done is appropriately effective and constructive?

913. Are adequate and conveniently located toilet facilities available for use by the employees?

914. How are you auditing your organizations compliance with regulations?

915. If your organization thinks it is doing something well, can it prove this?

916. Have personnel cleanliness and health requirements been established?

917. Is there a risk that information provided by management may not always be reliable?

918. Health and safety arrangements; stress management workshops. How does your organization know that it provides a safe and healthy environment?

919. Does the audit organization have experience in performing the required work for entities of your type and size?

3.6 Team Directory: ISO 20000

920. Contract requirements complied with?

921. When will you produce deliverables?

922. Does a ISO 20000 project team directory list all resources assigned to the ISO 20000 project?

923. Decisions: what could be done better to improve the quality of the constructed product?

924. Who will be the stakeholders on your next ISO 20000 project?

925. What needs to be communicated?

926. Process decisions: is work progressing on schedule and per contract requirements?

927. Who are the Team Members?

928. Process decisions: do job conditions warrant additional actions to collect job information and document on-site activity?

929. What are you going to deliver or accomplish?

930. How will you accomplish and manage the objectives?

931. Do purchase specifications and configurations match requirements?

932. When does information need to be distributed?

933. How do unidentified risks impact the outcome of the ISO 20000 project?

934. Who will write the meeting minutes and distribute?

935. Who will report ISO 20000 project status to all stakeholders?

936. Days from the time the issue is identified?

937. Have you decided when to celebrate the ISO 20000 projects completion date?

3.7 Team Operating Agreement: ISO 20000

938. What individual strengths does each team member bring to the group?

939. Do you begin with a question to engage everyone?

940. Do you vary your voice pace, tone and pitch to engage participants and gain involvement?

941. How will your group handle planned absences?

942. What resources can be provided for the team in terms of equipment, space, time for training, protected time and space for meetings, and travel allowances?

943. Do you upload presentation materials in advance and test the technology?

944. Do team members reside in more than two countries?

945. Methodologies: how will key team processes be implemented, such as training, research, work deliverable production, review and approval processes, knowledge management, and meeting procedures?

946. Do you record meetings for the already stated unable to attend?

947. Has the appropriate access to relevant data and analysis capability been granted?

948. Communication protocols: how will the team communicate?

949. Seconds for members to respond?

950. Do you solicit member feedback about meetings and what would make them better?

951. Do you determine the meeting length and time of day?

952. What are the boundaries (organizational or geographic) within which you operate?

953. Are there influences outside the team that may affect performance, and if so, have you identified and addressed them?

954. How will group handle unplanned absences?

955. What administrative supports will be put in place to support the team and the teams supervisor?

956. Do team members need to frequently communicate as a full group to make timely decisions?

957. To whom do you deliver your services?

3.8 Team Performance Assessment: ISO 20000

958. Delaying market entry: how long is too long?

959. How do you recognize and praise members for contributions?

960. To what degree are the relative importance and priority of the goals clear to all team members?

961. To what degree does the teams purpose contain themes that are particularly meaningful and memorable?

962. If you have criticized someones work for method variance in your role as reviewer, what was the circumstance?

963. To what degree will team members, individually and collectively, commit time to help themselves and others learn and develop skills?

964. What structural changes have you made or are you preparing to make?

965. Does more radicalness mean more perceived benefits?

966. To what degree do members understand and articulate the same purpose without relying on ambiguous abstractions?

967. To what degree will new and supplemental skills be introduced as the need is recognized?

968. To what degree does the teams approach to its work allow for modification and improvement over time?

969. If you have received criticism from reviewers that your work suffered from method variance, what was the circumstance?

970. To what degree are the goals realistic?

971. To what degree will the team ensure that all members equitably share the work essential to the success of the team?

972. Do you promptly inform members about major developments that may affect them?

973. To what degree does the teams work approach provide opportunity for members to engage in open interaction?

974. Where to from here?

975. What are you doing specifically to develop the leaders around you?

976. To what degree does the teams purpose constitute a broader, deeper aspiration than just accomplishing short-term goals?

977. Do friends perform better than acquaintances?

3.9 Team Member Performance Assessment: ISO 20000

978. How do you work together to improve teaching and learning?

979. What are they responsible for?

980. What are the evaluation strategies (e.g., reaction, learning, behavior, results) used. What evaluation results did you have?

981. How should adaptive assessments be implemented?

982. How will they be formed?

983. To what degree does the team possess adequate membership to achieve its ends?

984. What are acceptable governance changes?

985. To what degree do all members feel responsible for all agreed-upon measures?

986. In what areas would you like to concentrate your knowledge and resources?

987. How are performance measures and associated incentives developed?

988. Does adaptive training work?

989. What qualities does a successful Team leader possess?

990. Do the goals support your organizations goals?

991. Why were corresponding selected?

992. How are training activities developed from a technical perspective?

993. To what degree is the team cognizant of small wins to be celebrated along the way?

994. How are assessments designed, delivered, and otherwise used to maximize training?

995. What are the staffs preferences for training on technology-based platforms?

996. To what degree do the goals specify concrete team work products?

997. To what degree are sub-teams possible or necessary?

3.10 Issue Log: ISO 20000

998. Why do you manage human resources?

999. Who are the members of the governing body?

1000. Is the issue log kept in a safe place?

1001. How is this initiative related to other portfolios, programs, or ISO 20000 projects?

1002. How were past initiatives successful?

1003. What date was the issue resolved?

1004. Who is involved as you identify stakeholders?

1005. Which stakeholders can influence others?

1006. What is a change?

1007. How do you manage human resources?

1008. Who is the issue assigned to?

1009. What is the status of the issue?

1010. Is access to the Issue Log controlled?

1011. Who reported the issue?

1012. In classifying stakeholders, which approach to do so are you using?

1013. Do you have members of your team responsible for certain stakeholders?

4.0 Monitoring and Controlling Process Group: ISO 20000

1014. Is there adequate validation on required fields?

1015. How can you monitor progress?

1016. How were collaborations developed, and how are they sustained?

1017. What are the goals of the program?

1018. What is the timeline?

1019. What will you do to minimize the impact should a risk event occur?

1020. Who needs to be engaged upfront to ensure use of results?

1021. What were things that you did very well and want to do the same again on the next ISO 20000 project?

1022. When will the ISO 20000 project be done?

1023. Just how important is your work to the overall success of the ISO 20000 project?

1024. Propriety: who needs to be involved in the evaluation to be ethical?

1025. Is the program in place as intended?

1026. Is the schedule for the set products being met?

1027. How do you monitor progress?

1028. Change, where should you look for problems?

1029. Is there sufficient time allotted between the general system design and the detailed system design phases?

4.1 Project Performance Report: ISO 20000

1030. To what degree do team members articulate the teams work approach?

1031. To what degree are fresh input and perspectives systematically caught and added (for example, through information and analysis, new members, and senior sponsors)?

1032. To what degree are the goals ambitious?

1033. To what degree can all members engage in open and interactive considerations?

1034. To what degree are the structures of the formal organization consistent with the behaviors in the informal organization?

1035. To what degree can the cognitive capacity of individuals accommodate the flow of information?

1036. To what degree can team members meet frequently enough to accomplish the teams ends?

1037. To what degree does the teams work approach provide opportunity for members to engage in fact-based problem solving?

1038. To what degree do the structures of the formal organization motivate taskrelevant behavior and facilitate task completion?

1039. To what degree are the demands of the task compatible with and converge with the relationships of the informal organization?

1040. To what degree do members articulate the goals beyond the team membership?

1041. What is the PRS?

1042. To what degree is there centralized control of information sharing?

1043. To what degree will the approach capitalize on and enhance the skills of all team members in a manner that takes into consideration other demands on members of the team?

4.2 Variance Analysis: ISO 20000

1044. What are the actual costs to date?

1045. What is the performance to date and material commitment?

1046. What is the total budget for the ISO 20000 project (including estimates for authorized and unpriced work)?

1047. Historical experience?

1048. Are there changes in the overhead pool and/or organization structures?

1049. Are the actual costs used for variance analysis reconcilable with data from the accounting system?

1050. Are procedures for variance analysis documented and consistently applied at the control account level and selected WBS and organizational levels at least monthly as a routine task?

1051. Are material costs reported within the same period as that in which BCWP is earned for that material?

1052. Are your organizations and items of cost assigned to each pool identified?

1053. Did a new competitor enter the market?

1054. Is all contract work included in the CWBS?

1055. Are authorized changes being incorporated in a timely manner?

1056. What business event caused the fluctuation?

1057. Who is generally responsible for monitoring and taking action on variances?

1058. Is work progressively subdivided into detailed work packages as requirements are defined?

1059. Are control accounts opened and closed based on the start and completion of work contained therein?

1060. Are the bases and rates for allocating costs from each indirect pool consistently applied?

1061. Why do variances exist?

1062. What business event causes fluctuations?

1063. Is budgeted cost for work performed calculated in a manner consistent with the way work is planned?

4.3 Earned Value Status: ISO 20000

1064. Where is evidence-based earned value in your organization reported?

1065. How does this compare with other ISO 20000 projects?

1066. Earned value can be used in almost any ISO 20000 project situation and in almost any ISO 20000 project environment. it may be used on large ISO 20000 projects, medium sized ISO 20000 projects, tiny ISO 20000 projects (in cut-down form), complex and simple ISO 20000 projects and in any market sector. some people, of course, know all about earned value, they have used it for years - but perhaps not as effectively as they could have?

1067. What is the unit of forecast value?

1068. Where are your problem areas?

1069. When is it going to finish?

1070. If earned value management (EVM) is so good in determining the true status of a ISO 20000 project and ISO 20000 project its completion, why is it that hardly any one uses it in information systems related ISO 20000 projects?

1071. Are you hitting your ISO 20000 projects targets?

1072. Validation is a process of ensuring that the developed system will actually achieve the stakeholders desired outcomes; Are you building the right product? What do you validate?

1073. Verification is a process of ensuring that the developed system satisfies the stakeholders agreements and specifications; Are you building the product right? What do you verify?

1074. How much is it going to cost by the finish?

4.4 Risk Audit: ISO 20000

1075. Strategic business risk audit methodologies; are corresponding an attempt to sell other services, and is management becoming the client of the audit rather than the shareholder?

1076. For this risk .. what do you need to stop doing, start doing and keep doing?

1077. Are ISO 20000 project requirements stable?

1078. Are all programs planned and conducted according to recognized safety standards?

1079. What is happening in other jurisdictions? Could that happen here?

1080. Can analytical tests provide evidence that is as strong as evidence from traditional substantive tests?

1081. What are the risks that could stop you from achieving your KPIs?

1082. Have all possible risks/hazards been identified (including injury to staff, damage to equipment, impact on others in the community)?

1083. Do you have a clear plan for the future that describes what you want to do and how you are going to do it?

1084. What are the costs associated with late delivery or a defective product?

1085. Does the ISO 20000 project team have experience with the technology to be implemented?

1086. Is all expenditure authorised through an identified process?

1087. Who is responsible for what?

1088. Are all managers or operators of the facility or equipment competent or qualified?

1089. Are policies communicated to all affected?

1090. Are procedures in place to ensure the security of staff and information and compliance with privacy legislation if applicable?

1091. Do your financial policies and procedures ensure that each step in financial handling (receipt, recording, banking, reporting) is not completed by one person?

1092. Is the customer willing to establish rapid communication links with the developer?

1093. Number of users of the product?

1094. Should additional substantive testing be conducted because of the risk audit results?

4.5 Contractor Status Report: ISO 20000

1095. What was the actual budget or estimated cost for your organizations services?

1096. What was the final actual cost?

1097. What process manages the contracts?

1098. How long have you been using the services?

1099. How does the proposed individual meet each requirement?

1100. What is the average response time for answering a support call?

1101. What are the minimum and optimal bandwidth requirements for the proposed solution?

1102. Who can list a ISO 20000 project as organization experience, your organization or a previous employee of your organization?

1103. How is risk transferred?

1104. What was the overall budget or estimated cost?

1105. Are there contractual transfer concerns?

1106. If applicable; describe your standard schedule for new software version releases. Are new software version releases included in the standard maintenance plan?

1107. What was the budget or estimated cost for your organizations services?

1108. Describe how often regular updates are made to the proposed solution. Are corresponding regular updates included in the standard maintenance plan?

4.6 Formal Acceptance: ISO 20000

1109. Does it do what client said it would?

1110. Do you buy pre-configured systems or build your own configuration?

1111. Who would use it?

1112. What lessons were learned about your ISO 20000 project management methodology?

1113. What is the Acceptance Management Process?

1114. Was the sponsor/customer satisfied?

1115. How does your team plan to obtain formal acceptance on your ISO 20000 project?

1116. General estimate of the costs and times to complete the ISO 20000 project?

1117. Is formal acceptance of the ISO 20000 project product documented and distributed?

1118. Was the ISO 20000 project work done on time, within budget, and according to specification?

1119. What can you do better next time?

1120. Was the client satisfied with the ISO 20000 project results?

1121. What function(s) does it fill or meet?

1122. What are the requirements against which to test, Who will execute?

1123. What was done right?

1124. Was the ISO 20000 project goal achieved?

1125. Was business value realized?

1126. Do you buy-in installation services?

1127. Do you perform formal acceptance or burn-in tests?

1128. How well did the team follow the methodology?

5.0 Closing Process Group: ISO 20000

1129. What is the risk of failure to your organization?

1130. Is this a follow-on to a previous ISO 20000 project?

1131. Just how important is your work to the overall success of the ISO 20000 project?

1132. Did the delivered product meet the specified requirements and goals of the ISO 20000 project?

1133. What is the ISO 20000 project name and date of completion?

1134. Will the ISO 20000 project deliverable(s) replace a current asset or group of assets?

1135. What business situation is being addressed?

1136. What were things that you did well, and could improve, and how?

1137. Can the lesson learned be replicated?

1138. Did you do things well?

1139. How will staff learn how to use the deliverables?

1140. Were cost budgets met?

1141. How well defined and documented were the ISO 20000 project management processes you chose to use?

1142. If a risk event occurs, what will you do?

1143. How critical is the ISO 20000 project success to the success of your organization?

5.1 Procurement Audit: ISO 20000

1144. Are signature plates under the control of someone other than the individual given check-signing accountability?

1145. Is the procurement process fully digitalized?

1146. How do you ensure whether the goods were supplied or works executed in time and properly recorded in measurement books and stock/works registers after inspection?

1147. Was the outcome of the award process properly reached and communicated?

1148. Are regulations on taxes, fees, duties, excises, tariffs etc. not impeding (international) competition?

1149. Is there a policy covering the relationship of other departments with vendors?

1150. Relevance of the contract to the Internal Market?

1151. Is the procurement function/unit organized the most appropriate way taking into consideration the actual tasks which the department has to carry out?

1152. Are lease-purchase agreements drawn and processed in accordance with law and regulation?

1153. Are transportation charges verified?

1154. Did you consider and evaluate alternatives, like bundling needs with other departments or grouping supplies in separate lots with different characteristics?

1155. Is your organization aware and informed about international procurement standards and good practice?

1156. Was the pre-qualification screening for issue of tender documents done properly and in a fair manner?

1157. Is the issuance of purchase orders scheduled so that orders are not issued daily?

1158. Are all mutilated and voided checks retained for proper accounting of pre-numbered checks?

1159. Is the accounting distribution of expenses included with the request for payment?

1160. Did the additional works introduce minor or non-substantial changes to performance, as described in the contract documents?

1161. Were there no material changes in the contract shortly after award?

1162. Is the procurement process organized the most appropriate way taking into consideration the amount of procurement?

1163. Is the approval graduated according to the amount disbursed?

5.2 Contract Close-Out: ISO 20000

1164. Parties: Authorized?

1165. Are the signers the authorized officials?

1166. Parties: who is involved?

1167. Have all contracts been closed?

1168. Has each contract been audited to verify acceptance and delivery?

1169. Have all acceptance criteria been met prior to final payment to contractors?

1170. Have all contracts been completed?

1171. Why Outsource?

1172. Was the contract sufficiently clear so as not to result in numerous disputes and misunderstandings?

1173. Change in attitude or behavior?

1174. How is the contracting office notified of the automatic contract close-out?

1175. How/when used ?

1176. Was the contract complete without requiring numerous changes and revisions?

1177. What is capture management?

1178. Change in circumstances?

1179. Was the contract type appropriate?

1180. How does it work?

1181. What happens to the recipient of services?

1182. Have all contract records been included in the ISO 20000 project archives?

1183. Change in knowledge?

5.3 Project or Phase Close-Out: ISO 20000

1184. What are the mandatory communication needs for each stakeholder?

1185. Did the delivered product meet the specified requirements and goals of the ISO 20000 project?

1186. Is the lesson significant, valid, and applicable?

1187. How often did each stakeholder need an update?

1188. What are the informational communication needs for each stakeholder?

1189. Is there a clear cause and effect between the activity and the lesson learned?

1190. Who are the ISO 20000 project stakeholders and what are roles and involvement?

1191. Which changes might a stakeholder be required to make as a result of the ISO 20000 project?

1192. Did the ISO 20000 project management methodology work?

1193. Have business partners been involved extensively, and what data was required for them?

1194. Is the lesson based on actual ISO 20000 project

experience rather than on independent research?

1195. Does the lesson describe a function that would be done differently the next time?

1196. What information did each stakeholder need to contribute to the ISO 20000 projects success?

1197. What were the desired outcomes?

1198. What was the preferred delivery mechanism?

1199. Who is responsible for award close-out?

1200. Were messages directly related to the release strategy or phases of the ISO 20000 project?

1201. What can you do better next time, and what specific actions can you take to improve?

1202. What is a Risk?

5.4 Lessons Learned: ISO 20000

1203. What were the problems encountered in the ISO 20000 project-functional area relationship, why, and how could they be fixed?

1204. What were the major enablers to a quick response?

1205. Were any strategies or activities unsuccessful?

1206. How effective were Best Practices & Lessons Learned from prior ISO 20000 projects utilized in this ISO 20000 project?

1207. Was ISO 20000 project performance validated or challenged?

1208. How much communication is socially oriented?

1209. How do individuals resolve conflict?

1210. Whom to share Lessons Learned Information with?

1211. What is your strategy for data collection?

1212. Do you have any real problems?

1213. How effectively were issues resolved before escalation was necessary?

1214. What is the fiscal dependency?

1215. How many government and contractor personnel are authorized for the ISO 20000 project?

1216. If issue escalation was required, how effectively were issues resolved?

1217. What is the impact of tax policy on the case?

1218. What is the expected lifespan of the deliverable?

1219. What surprises did the team have to deal with?

1220. Do you conduct the engineering tests?

1221. If you had to do this ISO 20000 project again, what is the one thing that you would change (related to process, not to technical solutions)?

1222. Would you spend your own money to fix this issue?

Index

Printed in Great Britain
by Amazon